Painting Flea Market Furniture

Painting Flea Market Furniture

Kathryn Elliott

Sterling Publishing Co., Inc.
New York
A Sterling / Chapelle Book

Library of Congress Cataloging-in-Publication Data Available

Chapelle, Ltd:

Jo Packham, Sara Toliver, Cindy Stoeckl

Cathy Sexton, Editor

Karla Haberstich, Art Director

Marilyn Goff, Copy Editor

Staff:

Kelly Ashkettle, Areta Bingham, Donna Chambers, Emily Frandsen, Lana Hall, Susan Jorgensen, Jennifer Luman, Melissa Maynard, Barbara Milburn, Lecia Monsen, Suzy Skadburg, Kim Taylor, Linda Venditti, Desirée Wybrow

Photography:

Ryne Hazen and Kevin Dilley for Hazen Imaging, Inc.

Dianne Dietrich Leis

Scot Zimmerman

If you have any questions or comments or would like information on specialty products featured in this book, please contact:

Chapelle, Ltd., Inc.
P.O. Box 9252
Ogden, UT 84409
(801) 621-2777 • (801) 621-2788 Fax
e-mail: chapelle@chapelleltd.com
web site: www.chapelleltd.com

10 9 8 7 6 5 4 3 2 1

Published by Sterling Publishing Co., Inc.
387 Park Avenue South, New York, NY 10016
© 2004 by Kathryn Elliott
Distributed in Canada by Sterling Publishing
c/o Canadian Manda Group, One Atlantic Avenue, Suite 105
Toronto, Ontario, Canada M6K 3E7
Distributed in Great Britain by Chrysalis Books Group PLC,
The Chrysalis Building, Bramley Road, London W10 6 SP, England.
Distributed in Australia by Capricorn Link (Australia) Pty. Ltd.
P.O. Box 704, Windsor, NSW 2756, Australia

Printed and Bound in China
All Rights Reserved

Sterling ISBN 1-4027-0725-8

Table of Contents

Flea Market Shopping

If it has been taken to the flea market or thrift store, it has got to be junk, right? Wrong! That fallacy alone keeps millions of penny-wise people out of secondhand stores. But, what many don't realize is that much of what you will find at these locations is an opportunity to transform outdated or worn objects into custom furniture pieces that will delight for many years. When compared to other costly options for furnishing your home, there isn't a better way to save money and develop your creative skills at the same time. Even if you don't have a flair for the artistic, there are simple ways to get a custom look without a lot of frustration. Half of the fun is the fulfillment you receive from creating something beautiful from someone else's throwaway.

In most thrift stores, there is a designated section for each type of used furniture. It would be helpful to check with the store management on when they restock their floor during the day. Knowing when you can return to the store to preview the latest supply of items can save you hours of wasted time.

If you are looking for a particular item, you may want to leave your number with the store management and have them call you if something close to your needs arrives at the store. For instance, I was looking for a twin head- and footboard to turn into a bench to place at the bottom of my son's bed. The store manager called to let me know they had received some that day.

Once in a while, you will run into retail seconds at the thrift store. This is a good opportunity to purchase up-to-date items that may not need as much work as the typical thrift-store treasures. The prices are considerably less than what you can even find at factory outlets, so don't let something you really like get away from you. If you think about it too long, it will be gone.

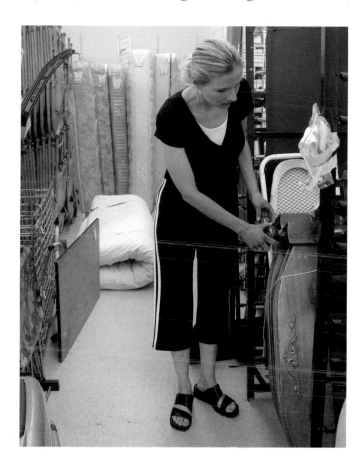

It takes a little time and patience to stroll through the aisles at the flea market; but with practice, you will be able to spot the swans swimming amongst the ducks. If you see something you like, take a look and inspect its condition. If it is irreparable, the time spent painting it will be a poor investment. Take your time investigating all the operational components. It is easier to discover them before you make your purchase so you can negotiate the price to cover the cost of the repair or rethink your purchase. As a rule, these items are not returnable.

Even if you don't know exactly what to do with a piece of furniture—get it now and play with it later, especially if you like it and it fits within your budget.

General Instructions

ANTIQUING WASHING

Mix two parts antiquing glazing medium with one part brown craft or flat latex paint. Working in a washing motion, apply the mixture with a very lightly dampened sponge over a previously painted surface.

This will give your painted surface a natural warm glow.

ACRYLIC-SPRAY SEALING (not shown)

Sealing any painted surface is an essential step in protecting it.

Following the manufacturer's instructions and standing approximately 12" away from the piece of furniture, very lightly apply the first coat of spray sealer. Apply as even a coat as possible to avoid dripping.

Lightly apply two or three additional coats. Let dry between each application. It is best to apply several light coats than it is to apply fewer heavy coats.

COLOR SMUDGING

This is a simple effect created with the use of oil pastel crayons. Simply apply the oil pastels over select areas of your painted surfaces and smudge them with your finger.

This technique can be used to create faux wood grain, surface shading, or coloring in areas that you would normally paint. Color smudges must be sealed with a matte-finish acrylic spray sealer.

This technique is good for use on areas that are small in size or detail, because coloring them in may be faster than painting.

COLOR WASHING

A color wash is prepared by diluting or watering down paint, and used to create a transparent shade of color. Apply the mixture with a sponge or clean rag over a contrasting color or finish to give the look of a transparent tint.

You may choose to dilute acrylic paint with a transparent glazing medium or simply use water to give a transparent characteristic to the paint. Start with a thin consistency, then thicken your wash by adding more paint, or apply additional coats until the desired effect is achieved.

COLOR
WEAVING

This blending technique incorporates loading multiple colors of paint onto a paintbrush. Place all of the colors into separate puddles on your palette, then dip the paintbrush into all of the colors at once. The paint is then blended together using a back-and-forth stroking motion until all of the colors are woven together into a seamless finish. The look of a woven fabric is the result.

Multiple dimensions are instantly added to your painted furniture when similar colors are applied and blended together.

CROSSHATCH
ANTIQUING

Mix two parts satin acrylic varnish or antiquing glazing medium with one part brown craft or flat latex paint. Apply the mixture with a 2" nylon paintbrush over a painted surface, working in a crisscross motion.

This will give your painted surface a heavy antiquing quality.

DECAL SHADING

Using a shadow tone underneath applied decals or stencils renders a unique three-dimensional effect.

Using a #2 pencil, carefully shade underneath decals or stencils where natural shadowing would occur. Stay consistent over the piece as if the light was all coming from the same source or direction. This will give a much more realistic shadowing effect.

After the shadows are drawn in, smudge all visible pencil lines with a smudging eraser.

DRY BRUSHING

Dry brushing is achieved by dragging an almost dry paintbrush that has been barely dipped into the paint over a constrasting surface to leave some of the prior finish showing through.

Pulling the paintbrush over the contrasting bottom layer in the same direction, and applying the slightest amount of paint to the paintbrush will allow you to work each consecutive paint stroke into where the last one ended.

This is a good technique to use when trying to achieve an aged finish. The end result will look like weathered wood grain, but do not limit yourself to using only natural wood colors.

METALLIC PEN LEAFING

Using a gold- or silver-leafing pen helps create metallic details with precision and accuracy. Lattice designs can be time consuming and difficult, but the use of a leafing pen makes the process easy and eliminates the frustration.

When precise lines are needed, mark and draw them first with a pencil, then trace over them. Let the ink dry for a few seconds before overlapping with a ruler or straightedge.

Lettering may also be done with a metallic leafing pen.

PAPER AGING

Making decorative paper look old and worn through a manmade aging process is a great method for covering flaws on furniture.

Crinkle the paper to be découpaged onto your piece of furniture, then open it up again. Get it wet and apply brown antiquing glazing medium over it with a sponge or paintbrush. While the paper is still wet, apply it to the surface of the piece of furniture with découpage medium. This will allow the brown tones to soak into the cracks of the crinkled, wet paper. Additional coats of antiquing glazing medium may be applied after the paper is dry.

SPONGE STAMPING

Sponge stamps can be found in various shapes and sizes, which makes for endless possibilities when stamping onto the surfaces of furniture.

Craft or flat latex paint is applied to the surface with a very lightly dampened sponge. Keep in mind the larger the shape, the more dramatic the results.

Varying effects are achieved by the amount of paint used in the application process. A light application of paint will render a soft, muted effect. A heavier application of paint yields a much more defined and intense design transfer.

Contrasting colors lend drama to the stamped surface. Applying the paint sparingly renders the best results, as globbed-on paint pushed flat onto a surface will not have accurate definition.

A small paint roller or a rubber brayer used to apply the paint to the stamp is helpful in achieving a more even distribution of paint in the application process.

SPONGING

This wonderful technique is employed by blending and muting two or more colors together with a very lightly dampened sponge onto a pre-painted surface.

The best results are achieved if the paint is applied from darkest to lightest. After the initial coat of paint is applied and allowed to dry, use the sponge to blend and mute the next lightest shade, working up to the lightest.

For more dramatic results, make the sponge marks more noticeable, allowing more of the distinct layers of paint to show through.

SPRAY-PAINT SPATTERING

This antiquing method can be used with either black or brown spray paint. To create a spattered effect, apply light pressure to the spray nozzle so the spray paint "spits" onto the painted finish of the piece of furniture. The hardest part is discovering at what pressure point the paint spatters instead of sprays.

This step may take a little practice to perfect, so try it on a scrap piece of paper until you have the confidence to proceed.

This technique is wonderful when used to mute intense or over-whelming colors.

STENCILING

Stencils are a versatile and effective way to achieve artistic content without a lot of freehand drawing abilities. Shapes and patterns can be created with the use of a cut-out design or form.

Once the design is drawn onto the surface, it can be colored in with paint, permanent markers, oil pastel crayons, or oil colored pencils.

For raised surfaces, stencils can be filled with wall joint compound. This adds incredible texture.

Another option for acquiring a textured look is to shade underneath stenciled areas or stencil decals. This will make them visually "pop" off the surface.

TAPING OFF

Painter's masking tape is the tool of choice for this technique. Measure off the areas you want to divide into separate stripes. The areas that are taped will avoid the adjacent colors you apply.

This is a timesaver for any design that must be precise. For more detailed designs, cut the tape with scissors or with a craft knife before or after it is pressed into place.

The advantage of using painter's masking tape opposed to craft masking tape is that it will not stick to previously dried paint surfaces or remove existing paint.

Projects

19

Botanical Nursery Dresser

This "ugly duckling" dresser was waiting patiently at the thrift store to be purchased and turned into a swan. The bottom of one of the drawers had fallen out; but all the parts and pieces were tucked away in the remaining drawers, which made the repair simple and quick. A little wood glue and two bar clamps was all I needed to pull the disassembled parts back together.

This dresser is the foundation piece for my granddaughter's nursery. Everything else in the room plays off the garden theme that has been executed by the freehand painting, découpaging, color-washing, ragging, and spattering techniques that have been applied to this piece.

The quickest way to personalize a piece of furniture is to write on it. First use your pencil to write your inscription, then trace over it with a permanent marker.

MATERIALS

USED DRESSER

100-GRIT SANDPAPER

CRAFT PAINTS: BROWN, GRAY, GRASSHOPPER GREEN, LIME GREEN, MINT GREEN, YELLOW OCHER, WHITE, BRIGHT YELLOW

3" FLAT NYLON PAINTBRUSH

1" FOAM BRUSH

SMALL-TIPPED DETAILING PAINTBRUSH

BROWN ACRYLIC LATEX SPRAY PAINT, SATIN FINISH

SMALL SCISSORS

WALLPAPER OR WRAPPING PAPER WITH A GARDEN THEME

WALLPAPER ADHESIVE OR DÉCOUPAGE MEDIUM

PENCIL

RULER

LEVEL

FINE-TIPPED BLACK PERMANENT MARKER

ACRYLIC SPRAY SEALER, SATIN FINISH

METAL BRANCH DRAWER PULLS

STEP-BY-STEP

1. Remove the drawer pulls.

2. Sand the entire dresser and remove any residue that could prevent the paint from adhering.

NOTE: If the used dresser is neither natural wood nor painted brown, you will want to sand it, then paint it with brown flat latex paint to achieve the desired results.

3. Load the nylon paintbrush with all three shades of green craft paint at once. Using a streaking motion and following the wood grain, apply the paint, allowing some of the original wood grain to show through. Let dry.

4. Sparingly load the beveled edge of the foam brush with yellow ocher craft paint. Using a sponging motion, shade all the edges of the dresser, including the drawer edges and the top. Let dry.

5. Sparingly load the tips of the flat edge of the nylon paintbrush with brown craft paint. Using a dabbing motion, create the "dirt" along the bottom edges of the dresser. Let dry.

NOTE: You may want to lightly sketch a reference line to follow.

6. Sparingly load the nylon paintbrush with all three shades of green craft paint at once. Using a fluid stroke, create the large leaf shapes extending up from the dirt. Let dry.

7. Sparingly load the tip of the detailing paintbrush with brown, white, and gray craft paints. Using a streaking motion and spinning the paintbrush as you cascade down the leaf shapes, create the veining effect.

8. Load the tip of the paintbrush with yellow ocher and brown craft paints. Lightly draw the paintbrush upward from the dirt to create the wispy wild grasses in the landscape. Repeat for additional patches of grass.

STEPS 3–4

STEPS 5–8

9. Using the foam brush, blend some foliage into the dirt, making certain to blend the bottom stalks of the leaf shapes and the grasses you have created.

10. Spatter the entire dresser with brown spray paint according to the General Instructions on page 16.

11. Cut the desired motifs from the wallpaper.

12. Determine where the cut-out motifs will be positioned on the dresser. Using the nylon paintbrush, apply wallpaper adhesive to the backs of the motifs, then adhere into position. Let dry.

NOTE: If necessary, they can be removed and reapplied.

13. Using the pencil, the ruler, and the level, lightly draw horizontal lines across the front of the dresser drawers where your chosen inscription will be written. Lightly write the inscription.

14. Using the fine-tipped permanent marker, trace over the inscription.

NOTE: The permanent marker will bleed slightly after the spray sealer is applied, so you will want to spread out your letters so they are still legible when your project is completed.

15. Seal the paint with spray sealer according to the General Instructions on page 10.

16. Install the metal branch drawer pulls.

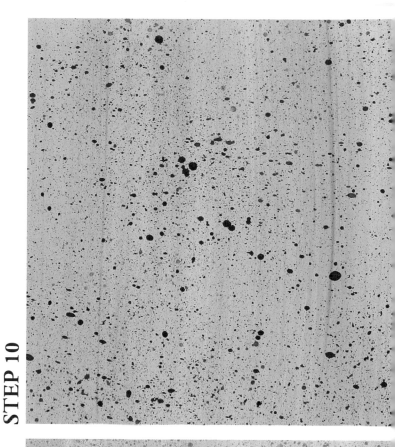

STEP 10

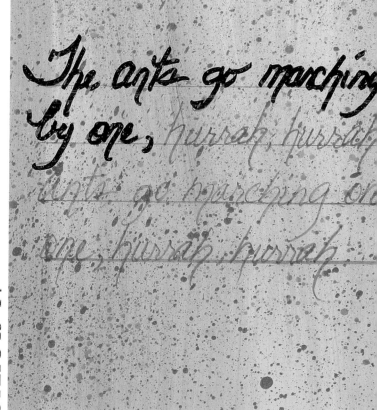

STEPS 13–14

Tricolored Changing Table

You need not paint everything in a nursery white to unify furniture pieces. This changing table is a perfect example of what a little color and a little ingenuity can do. I had plenty of the wallpaper border left over after I refurbished the Botanical Nursery Dresser as shown on page 21, so I incorporated the same garden theme and added some additional colors. This helped pull the rest of the nursery accessories together for a harmonious blend of form and function.

MATERIALS

USED CHANGING TABLE

100-GRIT SANDPAPER

CRAFT PAINTS: NAVY BLUE, GRASSHOPPER GREEN, LIME GREEN, MINT GREEN, YELLOW OCHER, BARN RED

3" FLAT NYLON PAINTBRUSH

1" FOAM BRUSH

SMALL-TIPPED DETAILING PAINTBRUSH

BROWN ACRYLIC LATEX SPRAY PAINT, SATIN FINISH

SMALL SCISSORS

WALLPAPER OR WRAPPING PAPER WITH A GARDEN THEME

WALLPAPER ADHESIVE OR DÉCOUPAGE MEDIUM

ACRYLIC SPRAY SEALER, SATIN FINISH

STEP-BY-STEP

1. Sand the entire changing table and remove any residue that could prevent the paint from adhering.

NOTE: If the used changing table is neither natural wood nor painted brown, you will want to sand it, then paint it with brown flat latex paint to achieve the desired results.

2. Repeat Steps 3–4 on page 22 to paint and shade the top of the changing table.

3. Load the nylon paintbrush with barn red craft paint. Using a streaking motion and following the wood grain, apply the paint to the top level of the changing table, allowing some of the original wood grain to show through. Let dry.

4. Repeat Step 3 above with navy blue craft paint to paint the bottom level of the changing table.

5. Spatter the entire changing table with brown spray paint according to the General Instructions on page 16.

6. Seal the paint with spray sealer according to the General Instructions on page 10.

Striped Accent Mirrors

It's always a luxury to find two exact items of anything at a thrift store; so when I saw these mirrors, I had to buy them. They were painted red, which would have worked well with the nursery décor, but I wanted to jazz them up a bit.

I used painter's masking tape to mask off sections, then I sponged between the tape with leftover white house paint. By simply peeling off the tape when the white paint was dry, I created even stripes without having to paint perfect lines. It was that simple!

MATERIALS

SALVAGED FRAMED MIRRORS

100-GRIT SANDPAPER

2" FOAM BRUSH

CRAFT PAINT, DESIRED COLOR

TAPE MEASURE

PENCIL

PAINTER'S MASKING TAPE

WHITE HOUSE PAINT

STEP-BY-STEP

1. If the frames on the salvaged framed mirrors are not already the desired color for your alternate stripe pattern, sand the frames and remove any residue that could prevent the paint from adhering.

2. Using the foam brush with the craft paint color of your choice, paint the entire frames. Let dry.

3. Using the tape measure and the pencil, measure and mark the stripe intervals.

4. Place painter's masking tape over the entire area at every other stripe interval. Make certain the tape is flush with the frame so the paint cannot bleed onto the other stripe.

5. Using the foam brush, lightly sponge white house paint between the taped-off areas. Let dry.

NOTE: Be careful not to saturate the edges of the tape.

6. Gently remove the tape and wipe away any excess paint on the mirror itself.

Contrasting-colored Rocker

As with most old wicker, the design usually has some raised areas that create visual interest. You can certainly paint it all the same unifying color, but why not call attention to those raised areas that were intended to stand out.

This rocker was a steal at $20.00. It had been painted white, and the paint was worn away in several places. Normally, I love a naturally weathered look, but I purchased this rocker knowing I wanted to use it in my granddaughter's nursery. I had already done most of her nursery pieces in a garden theme using red, blue, green, and yellow. The rocker would have looked good in any one of those colors, but using several of the colors together was the perfect accent to the existing furniture pieces.

MATERIALS

SALVAGED WICKER ROCKER

60-GRIT SANDPAPER

ACRYLIC LATEX
    SPRAY PAINTS, SATIN FINISH:
    NAVY BLUE, GRASS GREEN,
    BRIGHT RED, CANARY YELLOW

BROWN PACKING PAPER

PAINTER'S MASKING TAPE

BROWN ACRYLIC LATEX
    SPRAY PAINT, MATTE FINISH

STEP-BY-STEP

1.   Sand the entire wicker rocker and remove any residue that could prevent the paint from adhering. Wipe out all cracks and crevices in the wicker.

2.   Spray-paint the rocker entirely with red. Let dry.

3.   Using the brown packing paper and the painter's masking tape, mask off areas you want to paint with contrasting colors.

NOTE: The areas to be painted should be masked off with an adequate amount of paper and tape so any overspray cannot land on any other part of the rocker.

4.   Spray-paint the first area with blue. Let dry.

CAUTION: Make certain the painted areas are completely dry before moving on to the next area. This will ensure that the paint will not smudge or smear as the packing paper and tape are being removed.

5.   Repeat Step 4 above for the remaining masked-off areas with green and yellow spray paints. Let dry.

6.   Lightly spray-paint the constrasting-colored areas with brown to mute the colors and give the appearance of a timeworn patina. Let dry.

Wooden Floor Lamp

This floor lamp was a good match for the wooden sleigh crib we already had. The finish was slightly worn, so I simply distressed it a little more to further enhance its character. Certainly this is a time-saving alternative to refinishing.

Sponge painting on the neck of the lamp base spruced it up and a flea-market lamp shade was the perfect candidate for découpaging.

STEP-BY-STEP

CAUTION: You will want to wear safety glasses when distressing the wooden base on the floor lamp.

1. To distress the wooden base with dents and divots, strike the end of the chain against the wood.

2. Continue the distressing process by randomly striking the wood with the claw of the hammer until the desired result is achieved.

3. Cut a piece of construction paper to completely cover the neck of the floor lamp in excess of 2".

4. Using the scissors, notch out a small tooth pattern in the squeegee.

5. Using the patterned squeegee and tan craft paint, create a basket-weave or wicker pattern on the construction paper. Make a horizontal pattern across the construction paper.

6. Continue filling in the basket-weave pattern between the previously painted horizontal weave. Pick up the squeegee when you come to the horizontal lines and resume the pattern between them.

7. Lightly load the beveled edge of the foam brush with brown craft paint. Using a sponging motion, create the "dirt" along the bottom edge of the lamp shade. Let dry.

MATERIALS

USED FLOOR LAMP
    WITH WOODEN BASE

SALVAGED LAMP SHADE

SAFETY GLASSES

HEAVY CHAIN

CLAW HAMMER

SCISSORS

BROWN CONSTRUCTION PAPER

SQUEEGEE

CRAFT PAINTS: BROWN,
    MOSS GREEN, TAN

2" FOAM BRUSH

DÉCOUPAGE MEDIUM

CUTOUTS WITH A GARDEN THEME

COLORED PENCILS: BROWN,
    GREEN, TAN

SPONGE

METALLIC GOLD ACRYLIC LATEX
    SPRAY PAINT, MATTE FINISH

ACRYLIC SPRAY SEALER,
    SATIN FINISH

When you are browsing through the flea market, don't discount the lamp section due to outdated colors or styles. Oftentimes, these very same outdated lights make wonderful painting candidates.

This wooden floor lamp is a great example of how easy it is to give a wooden surface a quick-and-easy makeover. If you find a metal lamp, it can also be rejuvenated with a painted or antiqued finish. Applying a fresh new metallic finish, then aging with a patina is also an easy and dramatic effect to achieve. Even plastic and glass lamps can be painted—after being sanded and primed with an undercoat of matte primer.

Lamp shades can also be painted or decorated; but if the lamp shade is beyond a makeover, simply replace it with a more up-to-date version that will complement the newly painted finish of the lamp base.

8. Using the foam brush, apply découpage medium to the back of the construction paper. Adhere it onto the neck of the floor lamp. Let dry.

9. Apply découpage medium to the cutouts and adhere them into place along the contour of the painted dirt. Let dry.

10. Using the foam brush and moss green craft paint, lightly dry-brush over select areas of the faux dirt to create the illusion of foliage. Let dry.

11. Using the colored pencils, draw the wild grasses. "Root" the découpaged images by creating clumps of grasses underneath them.

12. Spray-paint the lamp shade with a very light "mist" of metallic gold. Let dry.

13. Using the sponge and brown craft paint, wipe over the wooden base of the floor lamp to fill in the distressed areas. Let dry.

14. Seal the paint with spray sealer according to the General Instructions on page 10.

Découpage and paint turned this ordinary lamp shade into a work of art.

Brown construction paper, painted in a wicker pattern with the help of a rubber squeegee and craft paints, lends a rustic flair to the neck of the floor lamp base.

Weathered Wooden Box

This wooden box has served many purposes in my décor. I had previously glued dried rose hips all over it. Those were removed and the dried glue had to be scraped off with a chisel.

Using a 1" nylon paintbrush, I washed over the rose-colored paint with three shades of green craft paint that I had thinned with water to give a more transparent consistency. By executing the color washing technique, all the previously painted layers were then able to show through and give the box depth of color.

Color-washing is an effective means to tie in a color scheme without having to completely change the color of a previously painted piece. Layered color combinations are endless and limited only to the reaches of your imagination.

Satin acrylic sealer does a good job of invisibly sealing and protecting, while allowing the dull-finish effect to remain.

Yard Clippings Dresser

Everyone who has a yard has some degree of yard and tree clippings at least once a year. Instead of grinding them up to use for mulch, try recycling some of them by hot-gluing them onto an unremarkable piece of salvaged furniture to transform it into a piece of art.

STEP-BY-STEP

1. Remove the drawer pulls.

2. Sand the entire dresser and remove any residue that could prevent the paint from adhering.

3. On a large area of floor space, map out a trial design with the yard clippings. Once you have achieved a desired pattern, hot-glue the clippings onto the dresser.

NOTE: Adequate clearance for the drawers must be considered.

4. Spray-paint the entire dresser with black. Let dry.

NOTE: Make certain to spray behind any raised objects that have been glued into position.

5. Using the foam brush and metallic gold craft paint, lightly brush over the yard clippings. Let dry.

6. Seal the paint with spray sealer according to the General Instructions on page 10.

7. Install the drawer pulls.

MATERIALS

USED DRESSER

100-GRIT SANDPAPER

YARD CLIPPINGS:
BRANCHES OR TWIGS,
SMALL PINECONES,
ACORNS, ROSE HIPS,
SEED PODS,
PINE NEEDLES

HOT-GLUE GUN AND GLUE STICKS

BLACK ACRYLIC LATEX
SPRAY PAINT, MATTE FINISH

METALLIC GOLD CRAFT PAINT

1" FOAM BRUSH

ACRYLIC SPRAY SEALER,
SATIN FINISH

You will never dread fall yard clean-up again after you see what can be done with the clippings. The pattern possibilities are endless, as are the materials you can use to embellish a piece of furniture using nature's bounty from your own backyard.

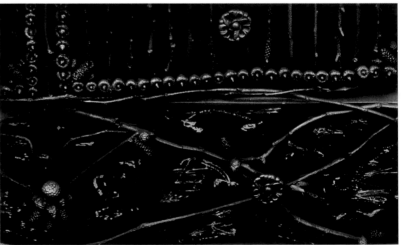

Letter-stamped Lamp Shade

This little project yielded a big impact. The lamps were purchased as a pair for $6.00. I needed a lamp to be used on the Yard Clippings Dresser as shown on page 35 that wouldn't eclipse the dresser's drama.

The lamp shade was an orphaned cast off given to me by my daughter. I was close to putting it in the throwaway pile, but reconsidered its fate when I went searching through my stash for a companion to the lamp base. Its simplicity complements both the lamp and the masculine statement of the neutral color scheme.

STEP-BY-STEP

1. Dust off the lamp shade so the paint is certain to adhere properly.

2. Place a small amount of black craft paint in the bottom of the cookie sheet. Roll the rubber brayer in the craft paint until it is evenly distributed on the roller of the rubber brayer. Load the vintage letter rubber stamp with the black craft paint by rolling the rubber brayer over the rubber stamp. Rubber-stamp the image repeatedly onto the lamp shade. Let dry.

NOTE: Because the surface of the lamp shade is curved, you will need to "roll" the rubber stamp to imprint the image in its entirety.

3. Continue embellishing the lamp shade by randomly stamping the vintage letters around the entire lamp shade. You will want some of the impressions to be less pronounced than others to make them look as though they have faded over time.

MATERIALS

SALVAGED LAMP BASE

SALVAGED LAMP SHADE

CRAFT PAINTS:
　　AMBER, BLACK,
　　METALLIC BLACK

COOKIE SHEET

RUBBER BRAYER

VINTAGE LETTER
　　RUBBER STAMP

1" FOAM BRUSH

100-GRIT SANDPAPER

BLACK ACRYLIC LATEX
　　SPRAY PAINT, MATTE FINISH

4. Using the foam brush and amber craft paint, lightly brush over the top and bottom trim of the lamp shade. Let dry.

5. Thin some amber craft paint to a watery consistency. Using the foam brush, wash over the stamped vintage letters on the lamp shade. Make certain to apply a heavier wash on selected areas. Let dry.

NOTE: The end result will be a muted yellow resembling an old faded letter.

6. Sand the entire lamp base and remove any residue that could prevent the paint from adhering.

7. Spray-paint the entire lamp base with black. Let dry.

8. Using the foam brush and metallic black craft paint, paint only the raised areas of the lamp base to give the lamp base the appearance of metal.

A throwaway lamp shade was rescued to complement the painted pewter base from the thrift store.

An oversized letter stamp was pressed onto the lamp shade, overlapping itself repeatedly, to create a literary theme.

A mist of gold spray paint warms the lamp shade to an old patina.

Moss-covered Frog

No fairy tale would be complete without a Prince Charming. Previously living in the front yard, he now resides happily in the nursery.

Raw concrete left outside in moist conditions will eventually grow moss. You can imitate that effect with craft paint, glue, and dried moss.

STEP-BY-STEP

1. Clean the surface of the concrete frog. Let dry.

2. Randomly dab moss green craft paint on the frog to simulate moss. Let dry.

3. Glue the dried moss over the painted areas. Let dry.

MATERIALS

CONCRETE FROG
    GARDEN SCULPTURE

MOSS GREEN CRAFT PAINT

ALL-PURPOSE GLUE

DRIED GREEN MOSS

Embellished Vintage Luggage

Luggage that has a wonderful timeworn patina can be transformed into practical and whimsical storage solutions throughout your home. These varied pieces of thrift-store luggage were transformed into a matched set, using decorative painting, spattering, stamping, découpaging, and antiquing techniques.

Old letters, stamp collections, and vintage postcards are great embellishments to use when découpaging any piece of luggage.

STEP-BY-STEP

1.   Old leather and vinyl luggage tends to have a dirt and grime buildup that may not be visible, but will prevent the paint from adhering to the surfaces. For this reason, you will want to thoroughly scrub the pieces of luggage with an abrasive cleanser.

2.   Lightly sand the luggage and remove any residue that could prevent the paint from adhering.

3.   Sponge white house paint over the luggage. Allow some of the original color of the luggage to show through. Let dry.

4.   Create your own stamped images for découpaging onto the luggage. Place a small amount of dark brown craft paint in the bottom of the cookie sheet. Roll the rubber brayer in the craft paint until it is evenly distributed on the roller of the rubber brayer. Load each rubber stamp with the dark brown craft paint by rolling the rubber brayer over each rubber stamp. Rubber-stamp the images onto brown packing paper. Let dry.

5.   After you have stamped several images, tear the brown packing paper around each of the stamped designs, creating irregularly shaped pieces with uneven, tattered edges.

MATERIALS

SALVAGED LUGGAGE

ALL-PURPOSE ABRASIVE
    CLEANSER

100-GRIT SANDPAPER

LARGE SPONGE

WHITE HOUSE PAINT

DARK BROWN CRAFT PAINT

COOKIE SHEET

RUBBER BRAYER

RUBBER STAMPS

BROWN PACKING PAPER

DÉCOUPAGE MEDIUM

3" NYLON PAINTBRUSH

CRAFT KNIFE

BLACK ACRYLIC LATEX
    SPRAY PAINT, MATTE FINISH

ANTIQUING GLAZING MEDIUM

CLEAN DRY CLOTH

ACRYLIC SPRAY SEALER,
    MATTE FINISH

6. Using the nylon paintbrush, sparingly apply découpage medium to the back of each of the torn pieces of brown packing paper. Randomly position them onto all sides of the luggage. Brush over the designs with a generous application of découpage medium. Let dry.

NOTES: Wallpaper border scraps also work well for decorative motifs. Adhere the pieces of border or cut-out images onto the luggage with découpage medium. Do this even if the border is prepasted.

If you have chosen to adhere the designs over the openings of the luggage, let the découpage medium dry completely. Then run a craft knife around the perimeter of the luggage to free the opening.

7. Reload the rubber brayer with dark brown craft paint, then reload each rubber stamp. Rubber-stamp the images directly onto the découpaged luggage, partially overlapping the stamped designs on the brown packing paper. Let dry.

8. Spatter the luggage with black spray paint according to the General Instructions on page 16. Make certain to spatter all the sides.

9. Mix the antiquing glazing medium with dark brown craft paint, following the manufacturer's instructions. Using the sponge, apply the glaze to the luggage in small manageable sections. Using the cloth, wipe away any excess glaze. Repeat with several applications until the result of a timeworn patina has been achieved. Let dry between each coat.

10. Randomly sand the edges around the luggage that would naturally sustain the most wear and tear.

11. Seal the paint with spray sealer according to the General Instructions on page 10.

STEPS 6–8

STEP 9

For added visual impact to your display of vintage luggage, reverse the color palette and paint the luggage black with white paint embossing. Pastels are also beautiful in a stacked arrangement.

Oriental Entry Console

This console was avocado green and although I liked the color, I wanted it to be a more dramatic piece. The console was $30.00 at the local flea market. The marble top was cracked on one end, but was easily repaired with some clear caulking adhesive. For added height and drama, I added resin corbels on the bottom, which cost $4.99 each at a discount store.

The recessed panels of the wooden doors were a wonderful launching pad for the stunning faux paint and découpage that ensued. I hung amber glass pears, purchased at the dollar store, between the corbel feet.

STEP-BY-STEP

1. Remove the hardware.

2. Sand the entire console and remove any residue that could prevent the paint from adhering.

3. Using the construction adhesive, adhere the corbels into place at the bottom of the console to serve as feet. Let dry.

NOTE: If desired, wood screws can be used to further secure the corbel feet.

4. Caulk around the edges of the corbel feet. Let dry.

5. Using the 2" nylon paintbrush and amber flat latex paint, paint the entire console, inside and out. Let dry.

6. Wet and wrinkle the color-copied photographs to distress them and give them an aged appearance. Carefully open up the photographs.

MATERIALS

USED CONSOLE

100-GRIT SANDPAPER

CONSTRUCTION ADHESIVE

RESIN CORBELS

ACRYLIC LATEX PAINTER'S CAULK

NYLON PAINTBRUSHES: 1", 2"

AMBER FLAT LATEX PAINT

COLOR-COPIED PHOTOGRAPHS

SPONGE

CLEAN DRY CLOTH

FOAM BRUSH

DÉCOUPAGE MEDIUM

PAINTER'S MASKING TAPE

SMALL-TIPPED
DETAILING PAINTBRUSH

CRAFT PAINTS: BLACK,
BROWN, METALLIC GOLD

COOKIE SHEET

RUBBER BRAYER

ORIENTAL LANDSCAPE
RUBBER STAMP

ANTIQUING GLAZING MEDIUM

7. Using the sponge and amber flat latex paint, wash over the photographs. Using the cloth, wipe away any excess paint, leaving a warm hue.

NOTE: If too much color remains on the photographs, run them under the sink faucet for a second to remove some of it. The photo paper will be fragile—do not try to wipe it with the sponge as it will tear very easily.

8. Using the foam brush, apply découpage medium to the backs of the photographs. Adhere them onto the console. Let dry.

9. Apply découpage medium to the backs of the embellishments. Adhere them onto the console. Let dry.

10. Select and tape off stripes along the bottom edge of the console with the painter's masking tape.

11. Using the foam brush, lightly sponge black craft paint between the taped-off areas. Let dry.

NOTE: Be careful not to saturate the edges of the tape.

12. Gently remove the tape.

13. Using the detailing paintbrush and metallic gold craft paint, paint between the black stripes. Let dry.

14. Using the 2" nylon paintbrush and black craft paint, paint the sides of the entire console. Let dry.

15. Place a small amount of black craft paint in the bottom of the cookie sheet. Roll the rubber brayer in the craft paint until it is evenly distributed on the roller of the rubber brayer. Load the oriental landscape rubber stamp with the black craft paint by rolling the rubber brayer over the rubber stamp. Rubber-stamp the image, repeatedly, onto the front of the console. Let dry.

16. Repeat Step 15 above using metallic gold craft paint to stamp the sides of the console. Let dry.

17. Using the 1" nylon paintbrush and metallic gold craft paint, wash over the trim pieces of the console doors and sides. Let dry.

18. Using the 2" nylon paintbrush and découpage medium, cover the entire console with short sweeping brush strokes to create a wavy texture. Let dry.

NOTE: The découpage medium will dry clear, making your piece appear oil painted.

STEP 15

19. Mix the antiquing glazing medium with brown craft paint, following the manufacturer's instructions. Using the sponge, apply the glaze to the console in small manageable sections. Using the cloth, wipe away any excess glaze, leaving a muted hue over the console. Let dry.

20. Apply additional coats of découpage medium over the edges of the photographs and embellishments as needed until all the edges are flush with the console surfaces.

21. Install the hardware.

Antiqued Rose Box

Once again a black background provides an eye-catching canvas for the painted rose design.
I looked at a picture of a rose and then sketched it with a pencil onto the black-painted wooden
box. I then painted the rose with select shades of red and mauve. I wanted the end result to be
a bit rustic so I didn't include a lot of detail.

The trim was also done freehand with the help of a straightedge. A coat of acrylic satin spray
sealer was applied for extended durability.

Whitewashed Bureau and Bed

MATERIALS

USED BUREAU

USED BED

LARGE SPONGE

ALL-PURPOSE ABRASIVE CLEANSER

BUCKET OF CLEAN WATER

100-GRIT SANDPAPER

ELECTRIC PALM SANDER

6" NYLON PAINTBRUSH

WHITE FLAT LATEX PAINT

ACRYLIC SPRAY SEALER,
    SATIN FINISH

This bed and dresser, though not from a set, were both good solid maple pieces of furniture. The bed was purchased for $5.00 and the dresser was a hand-me-down from a relative. The problem was, they were outdated in color and style. They both had good straight lines to work with, but not a lot of detailing to make them stand out in any way.

Since the intense red on the walls in this bedroom was the room's dominant focal point, I opted to keep the focus there and paint these two pieces of furniture in a subdued palette. This dry-brushing technique is easy, time friendly, and effective in unifying unrelated pieces into a harmonious color scheme.

STEP-BY-STEP

1. Remove the drawer pulls.

2. Using the sponge, give the wooden surfaces a good scrubbing with an abrasive cleanser. Over time, grime can build up on old pieces of wooden furniture, preventing a good paint adhesion to occur.

3. Using the sandpaper and the electric palm sander, sand the entire bed and dresser and remove any residue that could prevent the paint from adhering.

4. Using the nylon paintbrush and white flat latex paint, dry-brush the bed and dresser, following the natural wood grain. Allow some of the original wood grain to show through. Let dry.

5. Seal the paint with spray sealer according to the General Instructions on page 10.

6. Install the drawer pulls.

Some added whimsy was used in the form of ceramic rose-patterned drawer knobs. I had purchased an entire bag of thirty knobs at a flea market for $4.00.

I replaced the wooden handles on the bureau and drilled small holes in the tops of the short bed posts to insert the same knobs there.

I love how these little knobs customize these two pieces for just pennies.

Découpaged Desk

This desk was a homely one with no interesting features on it. With the help of some spray paint and a simple découpage technique, it was transformed into the charming focal point in a bedroom fit for a princess.

Salvaged handles, that were part of my collection of hardware, made the drawers more substantial and easier to operate. The old ones seemed too small for the weight of the drawers.

STEP-BY-STEP

1. Remove the drawer pulls.

2. Sand the entire desk and remove any residue that could prevent the paint from adhering.

3. Spray-paint the entire desk with barn red. Let dry.

4. Cut the desired decorative motifs from the wallpaper.

5. Determine where the cut-out motifs will be positioned on the desk. Using the nylon paintbrush, apply découpage medium to fronts of the drawers and to the backs of the motifs, then adhere into position. Let dry.

6. Sand the edges around the entire desk and around each drawer until the desired amount of distressing is achieved.

7. Using the foam brush and brown craft paint, lightly antique the sanded edges around the desk and drawers. Let dry.

8. Spatter the entire desk with brown spray paint according to the General Instructions on page 16.

9. Seal the paint with spray sealer according to the General Instructions on page 10.

10. Install the drawer pulls.

MATERIALS

USED DESK

60-GRIT SANDPAPER

ACRYLIC LATEX
    SPRAY PAINTS, MATTE FINISH:
    BROWN, BARN RED

SMALL SCISSORS

WALLPAPER OR WRAPPING PAPER
    WITH DECORATIVE MOTIFS

2" NYLON PAINTBRUSH

DÉCOUPAGE MEDIUM

FOAM BRUSH

BROWN CRAFT PAINT

ACRYLIC SPRAY SEALER,
    SATIN FINISH

Timeworn Victorian Highboy

This highboy is a perfect example of how many times you can transform a single piece of furniture with a little paint and ingenuity. In its first life, it lived in its original wood-toned finish in our dining room. In its second life, it lived in the bedroom of our daughter Chelsea, in this timeworn Victorian finish. It now lives in our guest bedroom as shown on page 83.

Instead of replacing the existing brass hardware, I antiqued it with white and brown paint, then sealed it. Now they also have a vintage appearance.

MATERIALS

USED HIGHBOY CHEST

60-GRIT SANDPAPER

ELECTRIC PALM SANDER

6" NYLON PAINTBRUSH

FLAT LATEX PAINTS:
    PALE PINK, WHITE

LARGE SPONGE

FOAM BRUSH

BROWN CRAFT PAINT

ACRYLIC SPRAY SEALER,
    MATTE FINISH

STEP-BY-STEP

1.   Remove the hardware.

2.   Using the sandpaper and the electric palm sander, sand the entire chest and remove any residue that could prevent the paint from adhering.

3.   Using the nylon paintbrush and white flat latex paint, heavily whitewash the chest, allowing a small amount of the wood layer to show through. Let dry.

4.   Using the electric palm sander, randomly sand the edges around the entire chest and around each drawer until the desired amount of distressing is achieved.

5.   Using the dampened sponge and pale pink flat latex paint, wash over the entire chest. Let dry.

6.   Using the foam brush and white flat latex paint, paint the hardware. Keep the paint from pooling around the moving parts of the handles. Let dry.

7.   Lightly antique over the painted hardware with brown craft paint. Using the sponge, wipe away any excess paint until the shade is a warm dark amber. Let dry.

8.   Seal the paint with spray sealer according to the General Instructions on page 10.

9.   Install the hardware.

The tops of furniture pieces such as this highboy are perfect for displaying and storing all kinds of pretty treasures. Accenting with vintage crochetwork adds a nice Victorian touch to your decorating.

Distressed-metal Grate

This ornamental grate was already chipped and peeling when I purchased it. It had even begun to rust slightly through the white paint in some areas.

I took a wire brush to it and removed the loose particles of paint in preparation to repaint it. The result of the naturally weathered metal was so charming, I couldn't bring myself to paint over it. Instead, I sealed the peeling, rusted surfaces to prevent any further rusting.

The vintage iron lantern chandelier was once wired for use, but the wires had been cut. I put candles where the lightbulbs would have been for a soft wall lantern. The pale pink color of the lantern is the original paint.

The vintage look created by pairing two seemingly unrelated objects together was a charming touch for a feminine bedroom ensemble.

Textured Dresser

This dresser was plain white and the top three drawers were missing. It had some pretty big dents and scratches that were going to be a challenge to cover. A coat of wall-joint compound, applied with a spackling spatula, filled all the imperfections and provided an interesting texture.

Wall-joint compound was then applied over a stencil and pushed into the stencil cutouts to create the relief on the drawer fronts and both sides of the dresser.

Baskets from the dollar store were found to replace the missing drawers. Vintage hardware that I removed from another salvaged piece of furniture made nice handles to easily access the new basket drawers.

STEP-BY-STEP

1. Remove the drawer pulls.

2. Sand the entire dresser and remove any residue that could prevent the paint from adhering.

3. Using the spackling spatula, apply wall-joint compound over the entire dresser in a crosshatching motion to create the reliefwork. Let dry.

4. Center the stencil on the first dresser drawer and secure it on the edges with painter's masking tape.

5. Cover the entire stencil with wall-joint compound, using enough pressure to push it down into the openings in the stencil. Smooth the compound to create a smooth surface.

6. Gently remove the tape and pull the stencil up from the corners. Let dry.

NOTE: If necessary, you may wipe off the compound and try it again. You will have to rinse any compound residue from the stencil and dry it off before repeating the process.

MATERIALS

USED DRESSER

100-GRIT SANDPAPER

SPACKLING SPATULA

WALL-JOINT COMPOUND

STENCIL

PAINTER'S MASKING TAPE

3" NYLON PAINTBRUSH

FLAT LATEX PAINTS:
    METALLIC CHAMPAGNE GOLD,
    MUSTARD GOLD,
    OFF-WHITE

OIL PASTEL CRAYONS:
    BLACK, BLUE, BROWN, GREEN,
    DARK GREEN, RUST, YELLOW

SILVER-LEAFING PEN

ACRYLIC SPRAY SEALER,
    MATTE FINISH

INDUSTRIAL-STRENGTH
    LIQUID ADHESIVE

7. Repeat Steps 4–6 on page 58 for the remaining drawers and for creating reliefwork on the dresser sides.

8. Once the reliefwork meets your satisfaction and is completely dry, gently sand off any rough or jagged edges to smooth the stenciled designs.

9. Using the nylon paintbrush and mustard gold flat latex paint, paint the entire dresser. Let dry.

10. Lightly dry-brush over the entire dresser with off-white flat latex paint, allowing much of the layer of mustard gold paint to show through.

11. Repeat Step 10 above with metallic champagne gold flat latex paint, allowing much of the previous layers of paint to show through.

12. Using the oil pastel crayons, color the raised areas of the reliefwork with blue, green, rust, and yellow.

13. Slightly smudge some of the color onto the flat dresser surface surrounding the raised designs.

14. Using the brown oil pastel crayon, color over the previous colors of crayon.

15. Slightly smudge some of the brown color onto the previously smudged areas to mute the overall effect.

16. Using the silver-leafing pen, smear silver over all the colored areas, allowing some of the muted, smudged colors to show through. Let dry.

17. Using the black oil pastel crayon, draw whispy branches on the dresser drawer fronts, sides, and top edges. Complement the black branches by adding some dark green oil pastel crayon.

18. Using the rust oil pastel crayon, color the edges of the dresser drawer fronts, sides, and top edges.

19. Using the brown oil pastel crayon, smudge over some of the rust-colored edges.

20. Slightly smudge the rust and brown colors to mute the overall effect.

21. Seal the paint with spray sealer according to the General Instructions on page 10.

22. Install the drawer pulls.

23. Glue the handles on the baskets.

For a smoother finish, lightly mist the wall-joint compound with a spray bottle full of water. The surface will be softer and you will not have to do as much sanding to get it ready for the color smudging.

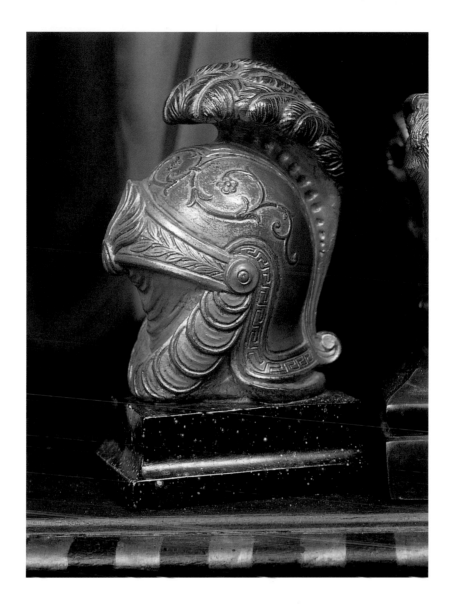

Faux-granite Bookends

These helmet bookends were $5.00 for the pair. They were painted in ghastly bright colors, so I turned them into ones with Mediterranean flair.

Black spray paint was used as the base color to cover up the original color. I then sponge-painted over the black with red, orange, and gold craft paints. The raised areas were highlighted with brown craft paint. Spray-paint spattering further enhanced the bookends. The final touch was creating a faux granite finish by painting "dots" of different sizes and color intensity with red, orange, white, and brown craft paints.

Chalkboard Chest of Drawers

This solution for a quick and inexpensive furniture fix-up is sure to please both young and old. Not only does it just get better with wear, it will save you substantially on handles, allowing those hard-earned dollars to stretch a little further.

This chest of drawers is solid pine so it was worth sprucing up. Nightstands, stacked on top of each other, can also be used as dresser "towers."

Because the paint is flat black, it makes a wonderful chalkboard surface for budding artists and cleans up easily with a spray-surface cleaner. Let the children label the drawers with chalk so they can easily identify storage drawers.

MATERIALS

USED CHEST OF DRAWERS

100-GRIT SANDPAPER

2" NYLON PAINTBRUSH

BLACK FLAT LATEX PAINT

ACRYLIC SPRAY SEALER, MATTE FINISH

ELECTRIC DRILL WITH 1" DRILL BIT

HEAVY-DUTY SCISSORS

1"-DIAMETER ROPE

STEP-BY-STEP

1. Remove the drawer pulls.

2. Sand the entire chest and remove any residue that could prevent the paint from adhering.

3. Using the nylon paintbrush and black flat latex paint, paint the entire chest. Let dry.

4. Sand the edges around the entire desk and around each drawer until the desired amount of distressing is achieved.

5. Seal the paint with spray sealer according to the General Instructions on page 10.

6. Drill through the existing holes in the drawers to accommodate the 1" rope.

7. Cut the rope into 12" sections.

8. Insert the rope ends into the drilled holes in each drawer and tie the ends in a knot on the inside of the drawers.

Medieval Vine Chair

This plain wooden chair got the medieval treatment with black spray paint and a gold-leafing pen. The same effect can be achieved with a small-tipped detailing paintbrush, but the pen cuts the project time in half.

Some tassels and lush pillows add to the old-world feel and make the chair look like a throne.

STEP-BY-STEP

1.   Sand the entire chair and remove any residue that could prevent the paint from adhering.

2.   Spray-paint the entire chair with black. Let dry.

3.   Using the #2 pencil, draw vines on the desired surfaces of the chair.

4.   Using the gold-leafing pen, trace the penciled vines. Let dry.

MATERIALS

SALVAGED WOODEN CHAIR

100-GRIT SANDPAPER

BLACK ACRYLIC LATEX
     SPRAY PAINT, MATTE FINISH

#2 PENCIL

GOLD-LEAFING PEN

A gold-leafing pen is the key to creating this conversation-piece chair. The vines were drawn freehand style.

A gold-leafing pen is also effective when you want to inscribe a favorite verse or anecdote on a piece of furniture or on the wall.

Silver-leafed Chair

This is a pretty great chair in and of itself, but it was a little too plain for my taste. A little silver-leaf sheeting took care of that rather nicely.

A guaranteed aged look is easily achieved with the silver leaf by applying the sheets and letting them split and tear. The wood finish on the chair will then show through, making it appear antiqued and worn. An antiquing glazing medium can be applied to the dried silver leaf to mute the silver luster.

MATERIALS

SALVAGED WOODEN CHAIR

100-GRIT SANDPAPER

SIZING BRUSH

METALLIC-LEAF SIZING

SILVER-LEAF SHEETING

1" NYLON PAINTBRUSH

CLEAN DRY CLOTH

ANTIQUING GLAZING MEDIUM

ACRYLIC SEALER,
    SATIN FINISH

STEP-BY-STEP

1.   Sand the chair where you plan to apply the silver-leaf sheeting and remove any residue that could prevent the silver leaf from adhering.

2.   Using the sizing brush, apply a generous coat of metallic-leaf sizing to the chair. The sizing will go on in a milky consistency. Let the sizing sit until it is clear and slightly tacky to the touch.

3.   Using the 1" nylon paintbrush, begin adhering the silver leaf, one sheet at a time, onto the tacky sizing. Brush away any excess silver leaf. Larger pieces may be saved to fill in vacancies where needed.

NOTE: To make the surfaces look worn, do not completely cover the wood with silver leaf.

4.   Using the cloth, wipe over the silver leaf with antiquing glazing medium. Make certain to apply a generous amount to the splits and cracks in the silver leaf. Wipe away excess antiquing glazing medium. Let dry.

5.   Using the 1" nylon paintbrush, seal the silver-leaf finish with acrylic sealer. Let dry.

Tortoiseshell Side Chair

I purchased this chair at the local flea market for $1.00. It is solid-wood construction with a flat-backed surface—perfect for a stunning feature.

Upon further examination, I noticed that some of the wood had chipped away along the top back edge. I sanded the chip and filled it with wood putty for a quick fix.

The ornamental iron along the seat bottom is composed of two metal plant hangers.

STEP-BY-STEP

1. Sand the entire chair and remove any residue that could prevent the paint from adhering.

2. Spray-paint the chair entirely with black. Let dry.

3. Lay the chair flat so the back is level with your countertops. To create the faux tortoiseshell, you will need a level surface.

4. Using the nylon paintbrush and brown, orange, red, and yellow craft paints, apply short strokes of varied color patterns to the seat back. Mute the painted streaks without completely blending them into the existing layer of paint. Starting from one side of the chair to the other, use a horizontal streaking motion in continuous, unbroken stroking patterns to create a more realistic foundation.

5. Carefully pour the denatured alcohol into the spray bottle. While the paint is still slightly wet, mist the surfaces of the seat back with the alcohol. The paint should start to "dimple."

6. Using the detailing paintbrush and black craft paint, paint dots of various shapes and sizes on the painted surfaces.

MATERIALS

SALVAGED WOODEN CHAIR

100-GRIT SANDPAPER

BLACK ACRYLIC LATEX
    SPRAY PAINT, MATTE FINISH

2" NYLON PAINTBRUSH

CRAFT PAINTS:
    BLACK, BROWN, METALLIC
    GOLD, ORANGE, RED, YELLOW

DENATURED ALCOHOL

SPRAY BOTTLE

SMALL-TIPPED
    DETAILING PAINTBRUSH

COLOR-COPIED PHOTOGRAPHS

FOAM BRUSH

DÉCOUPAGE MEDIUM

PAINTER'S MASKING TAPE

SCREWDRIVER

WOOD SCREWS

METAL PLANT HANGERS

ACRYLIC SPRAY SEALER,
    SATIN FINISH

7. Using the detailing paintbrush, drip small amounts of denatured alcohol onto the tops of each of the painted black dots. The black paint will begin to "pull away" from the alcohol, creating pools of variegated colors and shapes.

8. Repeat Step 6 on page 68 and Step 7 above with the remaining colors of craft paint until the desired results are achieved.

9. While the paint and the denatured alcohol are still wet, adhere the photographs. Using the foam brush, apply découpage medium to the back of the photograph you desire to use on the seat back. Adhere it onto the center of the seat back. Let dry.

NOTE: The pooling colors underneath the photographs will bleed through the paper and make the photograph appear as if it is a part of the tortoiseshell finish.

10. Using the foam brush, apply découpage medium to the back of the photograph you desire to use on the front seat apron. Adhere it onto the center of the seat apron. Let dry.

11. Select and tape off areas of the front seat apron with the painter's masking tape.

12. Using the detailing paintbrush and metallic gold craft paint, paint the stripes between the black stripes. Let dry.

NOTE: Be careful not to saturate the edges of the tape.

13. Gently remove the tape.

14. Using the screwdriver and wood screws, install the metal plant hangers under the seat of the chair.

15. Using the nylon paintbrush and découpage medium, cover the chair entirely. Let dry.

16. Apply additional coats of découpage medium over the edges of the photographs as needed until all the edges are flush with the chair surfaces.

17. Seal the paint with spray sealer according to the General Instructions on page 10.

18. Install the hardware.

STEP 7 (Black)

STEP 8 (Brown)

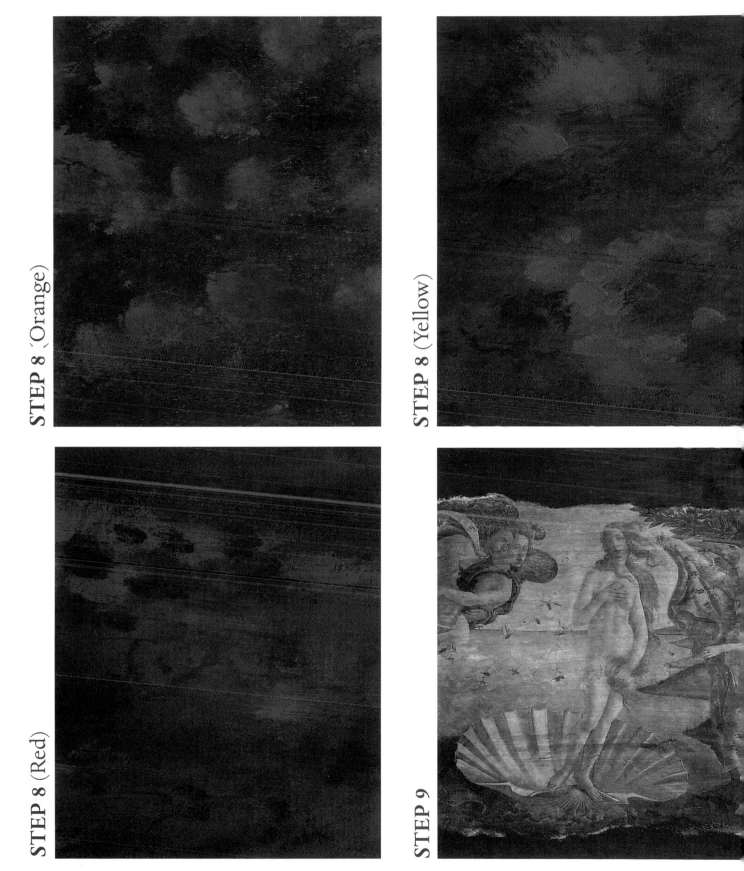

STEP 8 (Orange)

STEP 8 (Yellow)

STEP 8 (Red)

STEP 9

71

Traditional Spindle Side Chair

If you don't want to spend the time, effort, or money to refinish a wooden chair that has seen better days, give this simple solution a try. This chair is one of a pair that I literally retrieved from the neighborhood on trash day.

The wooden structure of the chairs was sound, but the finish was in desperate need of a makeover. This finish was achieved by lightly sanding the wooden surfaces, then painting them with black craft paint. The raised areas of the wooden frame were highlighted with metallic gold craft paint.

MATERIALS

SALVAGED WOODEN CHAIR

100-GRIT SANDPAPER

3" NYLON PAINTBRUSH

CRAFT PAINTS:
    BLACK, METALLIC GOLD

FOAM BRUSH

ACRYLIC SPRAY SEALER,
    SATIN FINISH

STEP-BY-STEP

1. Sand the wooden arms and legs of the entire chair and remove any residue that could prevent the paint from adhering.

2. Using the nylon paintbrush and black craft paint, paint the wooden arms and legs entirely. Let dry.

3. Using the foam brush and metallic gold craft paint, dry brush over the raised areas of the wooden frame. Let dry.

4. Randomly sand the edges around the wooden arms and legs until the desired amount of distressing is achieved.

5. Seal the paint with spray sealer according to the General Instructions on page 10.

Sponge-stamped Desk

This desk was a definite ugly duckling. It was plain light brown, very colonial, and pretty much void of any character.

My 13-year-old son had requested an orange and red bedroom with a tropical theme and I was lucky enough to have found a great sponge stamp, shaped like a tropical leaf, in the paint section of my local hardware store. We had found a pillow that incorporated the theme and colors that suited him and used it as the color inspiration for the desk.

The mismixed paint section yielded a great shade of hot cranberry and a bright orange—we were in business.

MATERIALS

USED DESK

100-GRIT SANDPAPER

3" NYLON PAINTBRUSH

FLAT LATEX PAINTS:
  BRIGHT ORANGE,
  BRIGHT RED

TROPICAL LEAF
  SPONGE STAMP

METALLIC CHAMPAGNE
  GOLD CRAFT PAINT

ACRYLIC SPRAY SEALER,
  MATTE FINISH

STEP-BY-STEP

1. Remove the drawer pulls.

2. Sand the entire desk and remove any residue that could prevent the paint from adhering.

3. Using the nylon paintbrush and bright orange flat latex paint, paint the entire desk. Let dry.

4. Dip the sponge stamp into bright red flat latex paint so only the raised areas of the stamp are covered with paint. Sponge-stamp the tropical leaf repeatedly onto the desk, overlapping the images and allowing some of the bright orange layer of paint to show through. Let dry. Clean and dry the sponge stamp.

5. Dip the sponge stamp into metallic champagne gold craft paint so only the raised areas of the stamp are covered with paint. Sponge-stamp the tropical leaf repeatedly onto the desk. Do not overlap any of the images this time, but allow some of the bright orange and bright red layers of paint to show through. Let dry.

6. Seal the paint with spray sealer according to the General Instructions on page 10.

7. Install the drawer pulls.

Wedgewood Side Table

Embossed wallpaper is the magic behind this delicate faux finish. The side table was in need of a total refinishing, but some blue and white paints saved me a lot of time and money.

STEP-BY-STEP

1. Sand the entire table and remove any residue that could prevent the paint from adhering.

2. Measure and cut the embossed wallpaper to fit the top of the table.

3. Using the nylon paintbrush, apply wallpaper adhesive to the back of the wallpaper and to the tabletop.

4. Adhere the wallpaper into position and work out any bubbles. Let dry.

5. Using the nylon paintbrush and the darkest shade of light blue flat latex paint, paint the entire table. Let dry.

6. Using the sponge and the lightest shade of light blue flat latex paint, lightly dab over the previous layer of light blue. Let dry.

7. Using the foam brush and white flat latex paint, lightly dry-brush over the embossed areas of the wallpaper. Let dry.

8. Seal the paint with spray sealer according to the General Instructions on page 10.

MATERIALS

USED SIDE TABLE

100-GRIT SANDPAPER

TAPE MEASURE

SCISSORS

EMBOSSED WALLPAPER

3" NYLON PAINTBRUSH

HEAVY-DUTY
    WALLPAPER ADHESIVE

FLAT LATEX PAINTS:
    TWO SHADES OF LIGHT BLUE,
    WHITE

SMALL SEA SPONGE

FOAM BRUSH

ACRYLIC SPRAY SEALER,
    MATTE FINISH

Create the look of blue wedgewood, using a piece of wallpaper border with a delicate embossed pattern painted with two shades of light blue, then sponged with white.

Leaf-stamped Side Table

This is a great side table of good quality that I purchased at the flea market for $20.00.

I love adding elements of nature to my painted furniture creations; it makes the pieces seem instantly comfortable. I also love black and try to incorporate it as much as possible. It makes such a great backdrop for all the colors used in this design.

A plastic fern leaf and colored pencils made this project an easy one.

STEP-BY-STEP

1. Remove the drawer pulls.

2. Sand the entire table and remove any residue that could prevent the paint from adhering.

3. Spray-paint the entire table with black. Let dry.

4. Using the nylon paintbrush and mustard gold craft paint, paint the tabletop. Let dry.

5. Using the medium-tipped brown watercolor marker, draw wood grain and "knots" on the tabletop to simulate natural wood.

6. Using the sponge, slightly dampened, lightly drag over the marker images to blur the wood grain and mute the knots.

7. Seal the paint with spray sealer according to the General Instructions on page 10.

8. Cut several various-sized fronds from the plastic fern. Place one frond on the ironing board. Cover the frond with a towel. Using the iron on the lowest setting, place the iron on the towel, applying heavy pressure over the frond. This will flatten the frond and make it suitable for use as a stamp. Repeat until all fronds have been flattened.

MATERIALS

USED SIDE TABLE

100-GRIT SANDPAPER

BLACK ACRYLIC LATEX
    SPRAY PAINT,
    MATTE FINISH

3" NYLON PAINTBRUSH

CRAFT PAINTS:
    BROWN, THREE SHADES
    OF GREEN, MUSTARD GOLD

MEDIUM-TIPPED BROWN
    WATERCOLOR MARKER

SMALL SPONGE

ACRYLIC SPRAY SEALER,
    SATIN FINISH

SCISSORS

PLASTIC FERN

IRONING BOARD

IRON

TOWEL

WATERCOLOR PENCILS:
    GOLD, GREEN

DÉCOUPAGE MEDIUM

ANTIQUING GLAZING MEDIUM

CLEAN DRY CLOTH

9. Dip one of the frond stamps into the darkest shade of green craft paint. Stamp the frond repeatedly onto the table. Apply equal pressure along the edges of the frond to make an even impression.

10. Repeat Step 9 above with the remaining colors of craft paint (except brown) until the desired results are achieved.

NOTE: The paint will not deposit in all the same places, which is the desired effect.

11. Repeat Steps 9–10 above, using the various-sized fronds to create interest. Let dry.

NOTE: It is not necessary to let the paint dry between each application of paint.

12. Using the gold watercolor pencil, draw spiraling tendrils emerging from the fern fronds.

13. Using the green watercolor pencil, enhance the design with undertones of green.

14. Using the nylon paintbrush and découpage medium, cover the entire table with crosshatching brush strokes. Let dry.

15. Mix the antiquing glazing medium with brown craft paint, following the manufacturer's instructions. Using the sponge, apply the glaze to the table in small manageable sections. Using the cloth, wipe away any excess glaze, leaving a muted hue over the table. Let dry.

16. Install the drawer pulls.

Practice stamping on a piece of paper with the fronds and the paint to see what the pattern will look like before you attempt this on the actual piece of furniture.

Urn Table

This urn already had a lot of character, but a little taupe paint washed over the surface areas, then wiped away, gave it more dimensional results. I slightly antiqued the raised areas with a little brown craft paint mixed with antiquing glazing medium. The glazing medium soaked into the "cracks" which made them even more pronounced.

A hand-stenciled platter turns the urn into a small serving-sized table perfect for chair and bedside service.

Stenciled Highboy

This highboy was originally stained in a cherry finish. It has been in the dining room, my daughter's room, and now it is living happily in the guest bedroom.

I had previously given it a distressed coat of white and pale pink. Leaving the whitewashed coat as the foundation for this new finish was a timesaver. The stripes on the upper half of the chest were done with a foam brush, painter's masking tape, and metallic gold craft paint. Mismixed paint in a great moss green color covers the whitewashed finish and accentuates the bottom half of the chest.

The detailing was made simple with the help of stencil decals, watercolor pencils, a gold-leafing pen, jewelry medallions, and small glass beads. Small-time effort for big-time impact—that's my kind of project.

MATERIALS

USED HIGHBOY CHEST

100-GRIT SANDPAPER

ELECTRIC PALM SANDER

3" NYLON PAINTBRUSH

FLAT LATEX PAINTS:
    MOSS GREEN, WHITE

PAINTER'S MASKING TAPE

FOAM BRUSH

METALLIC GOLD CRAFT PAINT

STENCIL DECALS

#2 PENCIL

GREEN WATERCOLOR PENCIL

WHITE GREASE PENCIL

RULER

LEVEL

GOLD-LEAFING PEN

GOLD-TONED
    JEWELRY MEDALLIONS

GREEN GLASS BEADS

SMALL FINISHING BRADS

GOLD-LEAF RUB-ON

A turned edge can be difficult to paint by hand. A simpler alternative is to wrap stencil decals around curved parts of furniture. After they are sealed, they become permanent.

STEP-BY-STEP

1. Remove the hardware.

2. Using the sandpaper and the electric palm sander, sand the entire chest and remove any residue that could prevent the paint from adhering.

3. Using the nylon paintbrush and white flat latex paint, heavily whitewash the chest, allowing a small amount of the wood layer to show through. Let dry.

NOTE: If the chest is divided into two sections, whitewash only the top half.

4. Using the electric palm sander, randomly sand the edges around the entire chest and around each drawer until the desired amount of distressing is achieved.

5. Select and tape off areas you want to stripe with the painter's masking tape.

6. Using the foam brush, lightly sponge metallic gold craft paint between the taped-off areas. Let dry.

NOTE: Be careful not to saturate the edges of the tape.

7. Gently remove the tape.

8. Adhere the stencil decals onto the front and sides of the chest, following the manufacturer's instructions.

9. Shade around the decals with the #2 pencil for a dimensional effect.

Decals tend to appear one-dimensional when they are applied to furniture. With the help of a #2 pencil, you can visually raise and lift the decaled designs. The dramatic difference it provides is well worth the extra time.

10. Lightly pencil-in the vines and trace them with the green watercolor pencil.

11. Using the white grease pencil, fill in the leaves.

12. Using the nylon paintbrush and moss green flat latex paint, paint the bottom half of the chest. Let dry.

13. Using the pencil, the ruler, and the level, make the lattice design on the bottom half of the chest.

14. Using the ruler and the gold-leafing pen, trace the penciled lattice lines. Let dry.

15. Place the gold-toned jewelry medallions on each lattic intersection. Secure with a glass bead and small finishing brad.

16. Apply the gold-leaf rub-on over the edges around the entire chest and around each drawer until the desired amount of highlighting is achieved. Let dry.

17. Install the hardware.

Lattice designs, drawn on with a gold-leafing pen, are an extraordinary accent to any piece of furniture. The trick is to carefully measure and mark the lines with a pencil before tracing with the gold-leafing pen.

Multifinished Chest

This chest is an authentic antique, but it had been kept in poor repair. The price tag of only $30.00 reflected its condition. Some of the damage to the wood was beyond repair, so it was a great candidate for new paint as a finish option.

This was one of those pieces that lent itself very well to adding other elements to spruce up its design appeal. Executing a variety of different finishes on the different layers of the chest helped create texture and interest.

The plaster plaques that adorn the sides of this chest were rescued from the thrift store. They were installed with construction adhesive, further secured with acrylic latex painter's caulk, then painted and gold-leafed.

MATERIALS

USED CHEST OF DRAWERS

100-GRIT SANDPAPER

TAPE MEASURE

SCISSORS

EMBOSSED WALLPAPER BORDER

NYLON PAINTBRUSHES: 1", 3"

HEAVY-DUTY
    WALLPAPER ADHESIVE

EMBOSSED GREETING CARD

ACRYLIC LATEX PAINTER'S CAULK

CONSTRUCTION ADHESIVE

ARCHITECTURAL ADD-ONS

BLACK FLAT LATEX PAINT

MARBLING PAINT KIT

SMALL SPONGE

CRAFT PAINTS: METALLIC GOLD,
    METALLIC PEWTER,
    TERRA-COTTA

SIZING BRUSH

METALLIC-LEAF SIZING

GOLD-LEAF SHEETING

GOLD-LEAF SEALER

PAINTER'S MASKING TAPE

FOAM BRUSH

GOLD-LEAF RUB-ON

ACRYLIC SPRAY SEALER,
    SATIN FINISH

STEP-BY-STEP

1. Remove the hardware.

2. Sand the entire chest and remove any residue that could prevent the paint from adhering.

3. Measure and cut the embossed wallpaper border to fit the front(s) of one or more drawers.

4. Using the 3" nylon paintbrush, apply wallpaper adhesive to the back of the wallpaper border and to the front(s) of the drawer(s).

5. Adhere the wallpaper into position and work out any bubbles. Let dry.

6. Cut the embossed design from the greeting card.

7. Adhere the design into place on the front of one of the drawers.

8. Caulk the edges of the wallpaper border and the embossed design to blend the seams into the drawer. Let dry.

9. Using the construction adhesive, adhere the architectural add-ons in place. Let dry.

10. Caulk around all the architectural add-ons. Let dry.

11. Using the 3" nylon paintbrush and black flat latex paint, paint the entire chest. Let dry.

NOTE: Additional coats may need to be applied for better coverage.

12. Using the marbling paint kit, paint the top of the chest in a faux marble finish, following the manufacturer's instructions.

NOTE: Several color options are available.

This wonderful engraving is actually embossed wallpaper border. Applied to the drawer and caulked around the edges, it should appear as if it was carved from the wooden drawer front and then painted.

13. Using the sponge and metallic pewter craft paint, lightly sponge over the black on the entire chest (except the top). Let dry.

14. Using the sizing brush, apply a generous coat of gold-leaf sizing to the desired areas of the chest. The sizing will go on in a milky consistency. Let the sizing sit until it is clear and slightly tacky to the touch.

15. Using the 1" nylon paintbrush, begin adhering the gold leaf, one sheet at a time, onto the tacky sizing. Brush away any excess gold leaf. Larger pieces may be saved to fill in vacancies where needed.

NOTE: To make the surfaces look worn, do not completely cover the wood with gold leaf.

16. Seal the gold leaf with the gold-leaf sealer. Let dry.

17. Select and tape off areas you want to stripe with the painter's masking tape.

18. Using the foam brush, lightly sponge metallic gold craft paint between the taped-off areas. Let dry.

NOTE: Be careful not to saturate the edges of the tape.

19. Gently remove the tape.

20. Using the foam brush and terra-cotta craft paint, lightly dry-brush over the edges of the entire chest and all the drawers. Let dry.

21. Apply the gold-leaf rub-on over the edges of the remaining embossed areas until the desired amount of highlighting is achieved. Let dry.

22. Seal the paint with spray sealer according to the General Instructions on page 10.

23. Install the hardware.

Wooden appliqués were adhered to this drawer front. A varied selection of wooden add-ons are available for a quick and inexpensive way to adorn a plain surface with a carved look.

Wheat-stenciled Table and Chairs

MATERIALS

USED TABLE AND CHAIRS

SPACKLING SPATULA

WOOD PUTTY

60-GRIT SANDPAPER

ELECTRIC PALM SANDER

3" NYLON PAINTBRUSH

FLAT LATEX PAINTS:
    GOLD, WHITE

STENCIL

PAINTER'S MASKING TAPE

STENCIL BRUSH

CRAFT PAINTS: GOLD, TAUPE

#2 PENCIL

SMALL-TIPPED DETAILING PAINTBRUSH

WHITE GREASE PENCIL

SMUDGING ERASER

ACRYLIC SPRAY SEALER,
    SATIN FINISH

The entire dining set was $40.00 at the local thrift store. It is wood, but it had some deep gouges in the tabletop. A little wood putty and, "voila." The gashes that would have disqualified this set from being a good refinishing candidate are now completely hidden under the painted finish.

Upon the initial examination, the pattern of the wooden slats on the chair backs resembled a wheat-stalk pattern. This was the inspiration for the stenciled wheat on the tabletop.

STEP-BY-STEP

1.   Using the spackling spatula and wood putty, fill any large gashes in the wood. Let dry.

2.   Remove the chair seats and set aside.

3.   Using the sandpaper and the electric palm sander, sand the entire table and all the chairs and remove any residue that could prevent the paint from adhering.

NOTE: Sand just enough to give an even surface for painting.

4.   Using the nylon paintbrush and white flat latex paint, paint the entire table and each of the chairs. Let dry.

5.   Randomly dry-brush over the white layer of paint with gold flat latex paint. Let dry.

NOTE: This will give the white paint an aged and yellowed appearance.

6.   Using the electric palm sander, randomly sand the edges around the entire table and around each of the chairs until the desired amount of distressing is achieved.

7.   Determine the placement of the pattern to be stenciled on the tabletop so the final design will be even around the table.

8.   Position the stencil on the tabletop and secure it on the edges with painter's masking tape.

9.   Using the stencil brush and taupe craft paint, fill in the design. Let dry.

The French motif stencil that I chose works well with the wheat theme as wheat is often associated with the French provincial regions.

10. Dry-brush over the taupe craft paint with gold craft paint. Let dry.

NOTE: This will make the stencil appear more dimensional.

11. Dry-brush over the taupe and gold craft paints with white flat latex paint. Let dry.

12. Using the #2 pencil, sketch out the wheat design on the tabletop and wooden slats of the chair backs.

13. Using the detailing paintbrush and gold flat latex paint, fill in the wheat kernels and leaves. Let dry.

14. Using the white grease pencil, highlight the gold areas.

15. Using the #2 pencil, shade all the painted wheat and stenciled designs. After the shadows are drawn in, smudge all visible pencil lines with a smudging eraser.

16. Seal the paint with spray sealer according to the General Instructions on page 10.

17. If desired, reupholster the chair seats.

18. Install the chair seats.

This was one of those times that the form of the piece dictated the outcome. The wheat theme was inspired by the pattern of the slats on the chair backs.

Mediterranean Serving Buffet

This cabinet once sat in a spare bedroom, void of any real character or function. One day I had the idea of transforming it into a serving buffet in deep rich colors with architectural add-ons.

What was once a $10.00 flea-market orphan is now the centerpiece of my kitchen.

STEP-BY-STEP

1. Remove the hardware.

2. Sand the entire buffet and remove any residue that could prevent the paint from adhering.

3. Using the construction adhesive, adhere the architectural add-ons in place. Let dry.

4. Using the nylon paintbrush and rust flat latex paint, paint the entire buffet. Let dry.

5. Select and tape off areas you want to stripe with the painter's masking tape.

6. Using the foam brush, lightly sponge metallic gold craft paint between the taped-off areas. Let dry.

NOTE: Be careful not to saturate the edges of the tape.

7. Gently remove the tape.

8. Using the detailing paintbrush and black flat latex paint, paint the stripes between the metallic gold stripes. Let dry.

9. Using the nylon paintbrush, apply short strokes of the black, brown, red, rust, and yellow flat latex paints to the entire buffet. Work in small sections so the paint does not dry before you have a chance to blend all the colors together. Do not let the paint dry completely.

MATERIALS

USED CABINET

100-GRIT SANDPAPER

CONSTRUCTION ADHESIVE

ARCHITECTURAL ADD-ONS

2" NYLON PAINTBRUSH

FLAT LATEX PAINTS:
    BLACK, BROWN, RED,
    RUST, YELLOW

PAINTER'S MASKING TAPE

FOAM BRUSH

METALLIC GOLD CRAFT PAINT

SMALL-TIPPED
    DETAILING PAINTBRUSH

DENATURED ALCOHOL

SPRAY BOTTLE

BLACK ACRYLIC LATEX
    SPRAY PAINT, SATIN FINISH

DÉCOUPAGE EMBELLISHMENTS

DÉCOUPAGE MEDIUM

ANTIQUING GLAZING MEDIUM

SPONGE

CLEAN DRY CLOTH

10. Carefully pour the denatured alcohol into the spray bottle. While the paint is still slightly wet, mist the surfaces of the buffet with the alcohol. The paint should start to "dimple."

11. While the paint and the denatured alcohol are still wet, spatter the entire buffet with black spray paint according to the General Instructions on page 16.

12. Repeat Steps 10–11 above until you are satisfied with the results. Let dry.

13. Using the detailing paintbrush and red and yellow flat latex paints, make small narrow streaks over the top of the buffet in a horizontal pattern simulating wood grain.

14. Using the nylon paintbrush, mute the red and yellow streaks without completely blending them into the existing layers of paint.

15. Repeat Steps 13–14 above over the front and sides of the buffet in a vertical pattern.

16. Wet and wrinkle the embellishments for découpaging to distress them and give them an aged appearance. Carefully open up the embellishments.

17. Using the foam brush, apply découpage medium to the back of the embellishments. Adhere them onto the buffet. Let dry.

18. Spatter the entire buffet with black spray paint according to the General Instructions on page 16.

19. Using the nylon paintbrush and découpage medium, cover the entire buffet with short sweeping brush strokes to create a wavy texture. Let dry.

NOTE: The découpage medium will dry clear, making your piece appear oil painted.

20. Mix the antiquing glazing medium with brown flat latex paint, following the manufacturer's instructions. Using the sponge, apply the glaze to the buffet in small manageable sections. Using the cloth, wipe away any excess glaze, leaving a muted hue over the buffet. Let dry.

21. Install the hardware.

STEP 9

STEPS 10–11

At first glance, the panels and shells appear to be molded out of the wooden serving buffet. They are resin plaques that were attached with construction adhesive, caulked, and painted to look like the rest of the richly hued cabinet.

Faux-wormwood Buffet

MATERIALS

USED DRESSER

USED HUTCH

100-GRIT SANDPAPER

3" NYLON PAINTBRUSH

FLAT LATEX PAINTS:
    BLACK, GOLD, WHITE

FOAM BRUSH

OIL PASTEL CRAYONS:
    BLACK, BROWN, ORANGE,
    RUST, YELLOW

ACRYLIC SPRAY SEALER,
    SATIN FINISH

I purchased this dresser at the local thrift store and this hutch at the goodwill outlet. I decided the dresser had great potential to be the base for the hutch.

My front room is a library and I needed more book and display space. This is a large piece, so it needed a wall of its own to really take advantage of its dramatic size.

I painted the dresser and hutch with a faux, rustic wormwood finish. The colors were chosen to make the most of the pieces without having it visually "swallow" the room. The lighter color palette is soothing, yet remains striking against the warm accents throughout the room.

STEP-BY-STEP

1. Sand the entire dresser and hutch and remove any residue that could prevent the paint from adhering.

2. Using the nylon paintbrush and white flat latex paint, paint selected areas of the dresser and hutch. Let dry.

3. Lightly dry-brush over the white layer of paint with gold flat latex paint. Let dry.

NOTE: This will give the white paint an aged and yellowed appearance.

4. Using the foam brush and black flat latex paint, apply the paint to desired areas of the dresser and hutch. Let dry.

5. Using the orange and yellow oil pastel crayons, highlight the edges of all the drawers and around the hutch.

6. Repeat Step 5 above, using the brown and rust oil pastel crayons. This will mute the orange and yellow highlighted areas.

7. Using the black and brown oil pastel crayons, draw the grain of the faux wormwood on the dresser and hutch.

8. Slightly smudge all of the colored areas to blend them.

9. Sand away some of the black painted areas, creating a distressed effect.

10. Seal the paint with spray sealer according to the General Instructions on page 10.

I was fortunate to have found this hutch with the great carving details already on it. If you aren't as lucky, use embossed wallpaper border or architectural add-ons to achieve this raised architectural detail on any piece of furniture.

The grain of the faux wormwood is created with the use of black and brown oil pastel crayons. The colors are then blended, or smudged, together with your finger.

Orange Tree Nightstand

This nightstand was a companion piece to the dresser that I used for the Faux-wormwood Buffet on pages 98–99. It was part of a set that I had purchased at the local thrift store.

Both pieces were going to end up in the same room, but I did not want them to look remotely related. I wanted each piece to be able to stand on its own character.

The warm accent colors in the front-room library dictated the colors on this piece. Some metallic copper craft paint really brings out the raised areas of the nightstand and the warm brown antiquing ties in the faux wood timbers I had just finished painting in the entry, which is adjacent to the library.

STEP-BY-STEP

1. Remove the drawer pulls.

2. Sand the entire nightstand and remove any residue that could prevent the paint from adhering.

3. Using the 3" nylon paintbrush, paint the entire nightstand with white flat latex paint. Let dry.

NOTE: This will act as a primer coat.

4. Paint the entire nightstand with bright yellow flat latex paint. Let dry.

5. Select and tape off stripes along the drawer fronts and the sides of the nightstand with the painter's masking tape.

6. Using the foam brush, lightly sponge metallic copper craft paint between the taped-off areas. Let dry.

NOTE: Be careful not to saturate the edges of the tape.

7. Gently remove the tape.

MATERIALS

USED NIGHTSTAND

100-GRIT SANDPAPER

NYLON PAINTBRUSHES: 2", 3"

FLAT LATEX PAINTS:
    WHITE,
    BRIGHT YELLOW

PAINTER'S MASKING TAPE

FOAM BRUSH

CRAFT PAINTS:
    BROWN, METALLIC COPPER

#2 PENCIL

FINE-TIPPED
    PERMANENT MARKERS:
    BLACK, BROWN,
    ORANGE, YELLOW

WHITE GREASE PENCIL

ANTIQUING GLAZING MEDIUM

ACRYLIC SPRAY SEALER,
    SATIN FINISH

8. Using the foam brush and metallic copper craft paint, highlight the raised areas on the nightstand. Let dry.

9. Using the #2 pencil, draw the orange tree motif on the top of the nightstand and down both sides of the front.

10. Using the fine-tipped permanent markers, trace over the motifs.

11. Using the orange permanent marker, fill in the oranges.

12. Using the yellow permanent marker and the white grease pencil, highlight the oranges.

13. Using the black permanent marker, create the navels on the oranges.

14. Using the brown permanent marker, mute the green leaves.

15. Mix two parts antiquing glazing medium with one part brown craft paint. Using the 2" nylon paintbrush, antique the entire nightstand, using the crosshatch antiquing technique.

16. Seal the paint with spray sealer according to the General Instructions on page 10.

17. Install the drawer pulls.

The orange-tree branches painted on the top of this nightstand were done using permanent markers that were sealed, then antiqued to mute the intensity of the colors.

Scenery Clock Art

This great clock is actually a molded plastic creation that I found at the flea market. The design of the piece really lent itself to playing up the detailing and form. I removed the clock hands and spray-painted the entire clock with metallic brass spray paint so I could start with a uniform painting surface. I then painted every other one of the twists on the braided side rails with a 1" foam brush and flat black craft paint. Using a sponging motion, I added flat gold craft paint with the foam brush to the inside recessed area of the clock, letting more of the metallic brass paint show through on the raised areas. The scenery painted on the clock face was painted freehand, but you can substitute a photocopied print instead to achieve similar results.

Decaled Louvered-door Shutters

These louvered doors were $4.00 for the pair at the flea market. They had previously been stained a dark walnut color, but were in need of an overhaul. I wanted a more rustic look in my library, so I stripped them of their existing hardware and used them as shutters on the library window.

The seashell swags on the fronts of the shutters were created with the use of stencil decals, which are available at craft and hardware stores. The handmade Mexican iron hardware helps carry out the rustic theme very well.

STEP-BY-STEP

1. Remove the hardware.

2. Sand each of the doors entirely and remove any residue that could prevent the paint from adhering.

3. Using the nylon paintbrush and white flat latex paint, dry-brush each of the doors. Let dry.

NOTE: You should have a "whitewashed" effect with some of the dark stain showing through.

4. Adhere the stencil decals onto each of the door panels, following the manufacturer's instructions.

5. Using the nylon paintbrush and mustard gold flat latex paint, wash over the white layer of paint and the stencil decals.

6. Using the foam brush and mustard gold flat latex paint, paint between the louvers and in the corners. Let dry.

7. Mix two parts satin acrylic varnish with one part brown flat latex paint. Using the nylon paintbrush, apply over each of the doors. If necessary, use the foam brush to get into the corners. Let dry.

8. Install the Mexican iron hardware and hang the shutters.

MATERIALS

USED BIFOLD LOUVERED DOORS

100-GRIT SANDPAPER

3" NYLON PAINTBRUSH

FLAT LATEX PAINTS: BROWN, MUSTARD GOLD, WHITE

STENCIL DECALS

FOAM BRUSH

SATIN ACRYLIC VARNISH

MEXICAN IRON HARDWARE

Carnival-striped Bistro Set

When I first laid eyes on this bistro set, it was absolutely pathetic. The tabletop was plexiglass and was badly scratched. The metal table and chairs had rusted and the white paint was chipping off. The chairs were covered in a lavender vinyl and were terribly sun-faded.

The table apron had this wonderful geometric design, as did the bottom of the chairs. I stood there looking at them until the flag pattern came into focus. I was immediately inspired to give the entire set a whimsical makeover with stripes painted in varied shades of mismixed paints.

STEP-BY-STEP

1. Remove the chair seats and set aside.

2. Using the wire brush, remove any chipping paint and rust from the metal surfaces of the entire table and each chair.

3. Lightly sand the table and chairs and remove any residue that could prevent the paint from adhering.

4. Using the caulk adhesive, secure the tabletop to the frame. Wipe away any excess and let dry.

5. Spray the table and chairs entirely with the primer sealer. Let dry.

6. Spray-paint the table and chairs entirely with black. Let dry.

7. Using the tape measure and the pencil, measure and mark the diameter of the table to determine the center. Using the pencil and the ruler, measure and mark the stripes, creating an even pattern.

MATERIALS

USED BISTRO SET

WIRE BRUSH

100-GRIT SANDPAPER

CLEAR CAULK ADHESIVE

BROWN PRIMER SEALER

BLACK ACRYLIC LATEX
    SPRAY PAINT, MATTE FINISH

TAPE MEASURE

PENCIL

RULER

PAINTER'S MASKING TAPE

FOAM BRUSH

CRAFT PAINTS, DESIRED COLORS

SMALL-TIPPED
    DETAILING PAINTBRUSH

ACRYLIC SPRAY SEALER,
    SATIN FINISH

8. Tape off the penciled stripes with painter's masking tape as you work your way around the table.

NOTE: You can only do several at a time because the tape will cover up the penciled lines.

9. Using the foam brush and the craft paint colors of your choice, begin painting the stripes.

10. Gently remove the tape as you paint each stripe.

NOTE: If the paint dries before the tape has been removed, it will pull away the paint on the edges.

11. Skip the next stripe so you don't place the tape over the wet paint.

12. Continue painting the stripes until you have completed your pattern. Let dry.

13. Using the detailing paintbrush, touch-up uneven lines. Let dry.

14. Repeat the taping off and painting method on each of the chairs.

15. If desired, reupholster the chair seats.

NOTE: Vinyl seats can be spray-painted.

16. Seal the paint with spray sealer according to the General Instructions on page 10.

NOTE: Make certain to apply a minimum of three coats of sealer for extended durability.

17. Install the chair seats.

The light installed in the center of the table was a great buy at $14.99. The streamlined style of the light matched this bistro set perfectly and it conceals the meeting point of the diminishing stripes. I simply drilled a hole in the center of the table to accommodate the cord.

Enchanted Forest Screen

Bring the outdoors in with a beautiful standing work of art created from bifold closet doors. The surface of the flat doors is a great alternative to canvas. The freehand painting on this screen is an advanced technique level. If you haven't yet acquired the confidence to master a large freehand work of art such as this, turn the screen into a huge collage of your favorite photographs découpaged directly onto the bifold doors.

MATERIALS

2 USED BIFOLD
    CLOSET DOORS

100-GRIT SANDPAPER

DROP CLOTH

SPACKLING SPATULA

WOOD PUTTY

WALL-JOINT COMPOUND

3" NYLON PAINTBRUSH

FLAT LATEX PAINTS:
    BROWN, GOLD, ORANGE,
    BRIGHT YELLOW

CRAFT PAINTS: DEEP
    JEWEL-TONED COLORS

PENCIL

ENLARGING PROJECTOR

ANTIQUING GLAZING MEDIUM

LARGE SPONGE

ACRYLIC SEALER,
    SATIN FINISH

STEP-BY-STEP

NOTE: Hollow-core or solid-wood door panels can be used in place of the bifold closet doors, but used bifold doors are a common flea-market item. When using door panels, it is best to use ones that are identical. However, the use of wall-joint compound for heavy texturing can be used to conceal unmatched doors. You will need to adjoin two door panels together with hinges and wood screws. Three hinges are recommended. It is also best to connect no more than two door panels for ease in moving them. More than two can become very heavy, which makes maneuvering them much more difficult.

1. Remove the doorknobs.

2. Lightly sand the bifold doors and remove any residue that could prevent the paint from adhering.

3. Place the drop cloth on the floor where you will be working. Make certain the drop cloth extends in excess of the width of the bifold doors.

4. Prop the bifold doors side by side in an upright position against a wall large enough to accommodate the width of the doors.

NOTE: You will want to find a wall in your home or garage where you can place the doors from start to finish. It is recommended that you not try to move the doors during the texturing and painting steps.

5. Using the spackling spatula, fill the holes in the bifold doors that were drilled to accommodate the doorknobs with wood putty. Let dry.

6. Using the spackling spatula, apply wall-joint compound over the entire door surfaces in a crosshatching motion to create a slight texture. Let dry.

NOTE: Make certain to work in manageable sections. Even the slightest raised areas will create a texture of varying degrees. The deeper the texture the more pronounced the antiquing will be because there will be deeper recesses for the antiquing medium to pool.

7. After the wall-joint compound dries, if there are areas that are too heavy, sand them down as desired. If there are areas that are too bare, add more wall-joint compound.

8. Lightly sand the entire textured surfaces to remove any sharp areas.

9. Using the nylon paintbrush with gold flat latex paint, base-coat the top area of the doors to create the skyline. Work some of the orange and bright yellow flat latex paints into the skyline.

10. Working your way downward to the bottom of the doors, blend a variety of deep shades of green to create the landscape.

11. Looking at a favorite landscape print, sketch the scene you want to paint onto the textured and base-coated doors. If necessary, use an enlarging projector to project the image onto the doors, then trace the scene.

NOTE: Enlarging projectors are different from overhead projectors. Overhead projectors are used only with transparencies. Enlarging projectors can be used with photographs, greeting cards, postcards, personal artwork, calendar prints, and pictures taken from any book or magazine. They are available in most craft stores.

12. Using the nylon paintbrush with the selected array of deep jewel-toned colors, paint the scene using your own sense of style and technique. Let dry.

13. Mix three parts antiquing glazing medium with one part brown flat latex paint. Using the nylon paintbrush, antique over the painted scenery, using the crosshatch antiquing technique.

14. Using a damp sponge, remove any excess antiquing glazing medium/flat latex paint mixture.

15. Using the nylon paintbrush, seal the bifold doors with acrylic sealer. Apply the sealer, using a crosshatching motion so the subtle finish replicates that of an oil painting. Let dry.

Italian Seascape Screen

A closer look at the detailing of this serene seascape reveals the texture created by the wall-joint compound used in this technique. Even though the color palette is soft and subdued, the overall effect is still very interesting.

Whenever you choose a more neutral color scheme, or there is a complete absence of color, you must rely more heavily on textures to create and stimulate visual interest.

STEP-BY-STEP

1.   Repeat Steps 1–8 on page 112 to prepare and texture the bifold closet doors.

2.   Using the nylon paintbrush with gold flat latex paint, base the top area of the doors to create the skyline.

3.   Working your way downward to the bottom of the doors, blend the taupe and white flat latex paints to create the muted seascape.

4.   Looking at a favorite seascape print, sketch the scene you want to paint onto the textured and base-coated doors. If necessary, use an enlarging projector to project the image onto the doors, then trace the scene.

NOTE: Enlarging projectors are different from overhead projectors. Overhead projectors are used only with transparencies. Enlarging projectors can be used with photographs, greeting cards, postcards, personal artwork, calendar prints, and pictures taken from any book or magazine. They are available in most craft stores.

5.   Using the nylon paintbrush with the selected array of neutral-toned colors, paint the scene, using your own sense of style and technique. Let dry.

6.   Repeat Steps 13–14 on page 112 to antique the doors.

7.   Using the nylon paintbrush, seal the bifold doors with acrylic sealer. Apply the sealer, using a crosshatching motion so the subtle finish replicates that of an oil painting. Let dry.

MATERIALS

2 USED BIFOLD
    CLOSET DOORS

100-GRIT SANDPAPER

DROP CLOTH

SPACKLING SPATULA

WOOD PUTTY

WALL-JOINT COMPOUND

3" NYLON PAINTBRUSH

FLAT LATEX PAINTS:
    BROWN, GOLD,
    TAUPE, WHITE

CRAFT PAINTS:
    NEUTRAL-TONED COLORS

PENCIL

ENLARGING PROJECTOR

ANTIQUING GLAZING MEDIUM

LARGE SPONGE

ACRYLIC SEALER,
    SATIN FINISH

Contemporary Room Dividers

These mahogany doors were $4.00 per pair at the flea market. I brought them home and removed the hardware. I had plenty of paint to do all the sides and edges in the different bright colors that I had used on the Carnival-striped Bistro Set as shown on page 109.

STEP-BY-STEP

1.   Remove the doorknobs.

2.   Lightly sand the bifold doors and remove any residue that could prevent the paint from adhering.

3.   Place the drop cloth on the floor where you will be working. Make certain the drop cloth extends in excess of the width of the bifold doors.

4.   Prop the bifold doors side by side in an upright position against a wall large enough to accommodate the width of the doors.

NOTE: You will want to find a wall in your home or garage where you can place the doors from start to finish. It is recommended that you not try to move the doors during the texturing and painting steps.

5.   Using the spackling spatula, fill the holes in the bifold doors that were drilled to accommodate the doorknobs with wood putty. Let dry.

6.   Sand the wood putty until completely smooth and remove any residue that could prevent the paint from adhering.

7.   Using the paint roller with the flat latex paint color of your choice, paint the entire door surfaces. Let dry.

8.   Using the nylon paintbrush with various colors of flat latex paint, paint the edges of each bifold door a different color. Let dry.

9.   Hot-glue the retro elements onto the bifold doors as desired. If the wood-putty-filled holes are not perfectly smooth, camouflage the imperfection by covering it with one of the decorative elements.

10.   Seal the paint with spray sealer according to the General Instructions on page 10.

MATERIALS

2 USED BIFOLD
  CLOSET DOORS

100-GRIT SANDPAPER

DROP CLOTH

SPACKLING SPATULA

WOOD PUTTY

PAINT ROLLER

FLAT LATEX PAINTS:
  DESIRED BRIGHT COLORS

1" NYLON PAINTBRUSH

HOT-GLUE GUN AND GLUE STICKS

RETRO ELEMENTS

ACRYLIC SPRAY SEALER,
  SATIN FINISH

Door Panel Valances

MATERIALS

USED 36" HOLLOW-CORE DOORS

TABLE SAW

WOOD

CONSTRUCTION ADHESIVE

DOOR PEDIMENT PLAQUES

ELECTRIC SCREWDRIVER

1" DRYWALL SCREWS

60-GRIT SANDPAPER

3" NYLON PAINTBRUSH

CRAFT PAINTS: BLACK, DARK BROWN

FOAM BRUSH

WOOD-GRAINING TOOL

ACRYLIC SPRAY SEALER,
    SATIN FINISH

CURTAIN RODS

DRAPERY PANELS

The backdrops are made from two 36" hollow-core doors. Each door was embellished with embossed wallpaper border, resin plaques, and mirrored tiles. The mirror helps make the door panels located on the vast wall look as though there is a window located there.

I put shelves over the top of the embellished door panels and secured curtain rods underneath them to hang drapery panels for a soft framing effect.

STEP-BY-STEP

1. Lay the door on a flat surface with plenty of maneuvering room on all sides.

2. Determine the layout of the wallpaper borders, resin wall plaques, and mirrored tiles.

NOTE: If you are making two or more embellished door panels, make certain each door is symmetrical so they look like a set.

3. Map out and measure the placement of the pine lattice strips that will frame and divide the decorative sections as described in Step 2 above.

4. Using the handsaw, cut the pine lattice strips and secure to the door with construction adhesive.

5. Measure and cut the wallpaper border to fit in the sections designated for the border.

6. If desired, distress the wallpaper border by wrinkling and dampening it.

NOTE: Make certain you do not saturate the paper as it will begin to tear where it has been creased.

7. Carefully open up each length of distressed wallpaper border and smooth it out.

8. Using the dampened sponge and metallic gold craft paint, lightly go over the surface of each length of wallpaper border. Let dry.

9. Using the nylon paintbrush, apply wallpaper adhesive to the back of each length of wallpaper border and position on the door. Let dry.

10. Using the construction adhesive, adhere the resin wall plaques into position on the doors. Let dry.

11. Using mirror adhesive, adhere the mirrored tiles into position on the doors. Let dry.

12. Caulk around all of the edges between the pine lattice strips, wallpaper borders, and wall plaques.

NOTE: Do not caulk around the mirrored tiles.

13. Using the nylon paintbrush and gold flat latex paint, paint the entire door, including all the embellishments. Let dry.

14. Using the table saw, cut the wood into a length that measures the door width. The width of the wood should be determined by your preference for the width of the valance.

NOTE: You will need one valance for each embellished door panel you will be hanging.

15. Apply the construction adhesive to the flat edge of the door pediment plaque and adhere it to the bottom front edge of the wooden valance. Using the electric screwdriver, further secure the pediment to the wood with wood screws.

NOTE: Let the construction adhesive dry completely before you begin the painting process.

16. Sand off any construction adhesive residue that may have seeped through the seams.

17. Using the nylon paintbrush and dark brown craft paint, paint the entire valance. Let dry.

18. Using the foam brush, apply the dark brown craft paint into all the cracks and crevices. Let dry.

19. Using the wood-graining tool and black craft paint, create wood grain to simulate a walnut finish, following the manufacturer's instructions. Let dry.

20. Seal the paint with spray sealer according to the General Instructions on page 10.

21. Using the electric screwdriver and wood screws, install the painted valance to the top flat edge of the embellished door panel.

22. Using wood screws, secure the embellished door panel to the wall.

23. Install the curtain rod inside the valance and hang the drapery panels at each side.

*A door, is a door, is a door, right? Wrong! If you develop door savvy you can
turn frequently discarded doors into a myriad of decorative accents for your home.*

Patina-finished Brass Urn

This urn was an unattractive brass pull-down light from the '50s. It had the cloth cord and everything when I found it at the goodwill outlet.

I loved the fact that it was brass, because one can do so much as far as weathering it. The products for this type of paint treatment abound at craft and hardware stores. This process actually etches and tarnishes the raw metal and varies in its results, depending on the type of metal being treated.

MATERIALS

SALVAGED BRASS
    PULL-DOWN
    LIGHT FIXTURE

100-GRIT SANDPAPER

CONSTRUCTION ADHESIVE

PLASTIC DROP CLOTH

FOAM BRUSH

WEATHERING MEDIUM
    FOR METAL

ACRYLIC SPRAY SEALER,
    SATIN FINISH

STEP-BY-STEP

1. Remove the electrical parts and pieces and discard them.

2. Sand the entire metal surface of the fixture.

NOTE: This is crucial, as most metals have a clearcoat to prevent them from rusting.

3. Using the construction adhesive, adhere the top ceiling-mount piece to the top of the lamp bowl. Wipe away any excess adhesive. Let dry.

NOTE: This will be the base of the urn so make certain it is installed to provide a flat, even resting surface.

4. Place the newly constructed urn on the plastic drop cloth. Using the foam brush, drip the weathering medium down the sides of the urn, beginning at the top, and letting it run down to the bottom. Let sit.

5. As the weathering medium sits, it will intensify in color. Wait to see the results of the first application before applying additional coats.

6. Once the desired color and tone is obtained, seal the patina finish with spray sealer according to the General Instructions on page 10.

Patched Cast-concrete Urn

This is a very heavy cast-concrete urn. When I bought it, I was not quite certain where I would put it; but for $3.00, I would take it home and decide later. It had been chipped in several places, so I filled in the areas of missing concrete with wall-joint compound, contouring the edges to match the rest of the urn's shape. When the compound was completely dry, I lightly sanded it to smooth the rough edges of the patchwork. Because I was going to paint it, the white patched areas weren't a dilemma.

The topiary inside the pot was made from dried fern branches purchased at the craft store. I salvaged a stick from my yard and drilled tiny holes in the top. I then placed a dab of hot glue on the tops of the fern branches and placed them into the drilled holes.

MATERIALS

SALVAGED URN

SPACKLING SPATULA

WALL-JOINT COMPOUND

SPRAY BOTTLE OF WATER

100-GRIT SANDPAPER

ACRYLIC LATEX
    SPRAY PAINTS, MATTE FINISH:
    BLACK, METALLIC COPPER,
    METALLIC GOLD

FOAM BRUSH

RASPBERRY CRAFT PAINT

ACRYLIC SPRAY SEALER,
    MATTE FINISH

STEP-BY-STEP

1.   Using the spackling spatula, apply wall-joint compound in the chips and cracks on the urn.

2.   For a smoother finish, lightly mist the wall-joint compound with a spray bottle full of water. Let dry.

3.   Lightly sand any rough edges remaining on the repaired areas of the urn.

4.   Spray-paint the entire urn with black. Let dry.

5.   Spray-paint the urn with a very light "mist" of metallic gold. Let dry.

6.   Repeat Step 5 above with metallic copper. Let dry.

7.   Using the foam brush and raspberry craft paint, lightly sponge over the urn, allowing much of the previous layers of paint to show through. Let dry.

8.   Seal the paint with spray sealer according to the General Instructions on page 10.

About the Author

An accomplished artist Kathryn Elliott is also a design consultant with over 20 years of experience. She has sold her paintings and custom-painted furniture pieces through art galleries in Palm Springs and Malibu, California. She currently works as a freelance decorative paint artist and muralist, as well as an instructor on faux and decorative paint techniques.

A published author, Elliott's first book "Junk Chic" was a Better Homes and Gardens Book Club bestseller. Within its pages, Kathryn takes the reader on an odyssey of exploration and discovery, turning junk into chic by combining her uniquely creative flair for art and design.

For the past two years, Kathryn has lent her expertise to "A.M. Northwest," an ABC affiliate morning talk show in Portland, Oregon. She was featured in an instructional decorating segment where she demonstrated a variety of design and decorating techniques. Kathryn's creative philosophy spread, as did her appearances on network and local television programs. In May 2003, she was a featured guest on the "It's Christopher Lowell" show. She is currently hosting a decorating segment on "Good Things Utah," on ABC affiliate KUTV.

Kathryn's follow-up book, "French Country Junk Chic," not only became an immediate bestseller in America, it is catching international attention as well. Elliott's books have enjoyed both commercial and critical success, creating a strong brand that is just the beginning in what is slated to become an exciting series.

Kathryn Elliott

Metric Conversion Chart

INCHES TO MILLIMETRES AND CENTIMETRES

MM-Millimetres   CM-Centimetres

INCHES	MM	CM	INCHES	CM	INCHES	CM
$1/8$	3	0.9	9	22.9	30	76.2
$1/4$	6	0.6	10	25.4	31	78.7
$3/8$	10	1.0	11	27.9	32	81.3
$1/2$	13	1.3	12	30.5	33	83.8
$5/8$	16	1.6	13	33.0	34	86.4
$3/4$	19	1.9	14	35.6	35	88.9
$7/8$	22	2.2	15	38.1	36	91.4
1	25	2.5	16	40.6	37	94.0
$1 1/4$	32	3.2	17	43.2	38	96.5
$1 1/2$	38	3.8	18	45.7	39	99.1
$1 3/4$	44	4.4	19	48.3	40	101.6
2	51	5.1	20	50.8	41	104.1
$2 1/2$	64	6.4	21	53.3	42	106.7
3	76	7.6	22	55.9	43	109.2
$3 1/2$	89	8.9	23	58.4	44	111.8
4	102	10.2	24	61.0	45	114.3
$4 1/2$	114	11.4	25	63.5	46	116.8
5	127	12.7	26	66.0	47	119.4
6	152	15.2	27	68.6	48	121.9
7	178	17.8	28	71.1	49	124.5
8	203	20.3	29	73.7	50	127.0

YARDS TO METRES

YARDS	METRES	YARDS	METRES	YARDS	METRES	YARDS	METRES	YARDS	METRES
$1/8$	0.11	$2 1/8$	1.94	$4 1/8$	3.77	$6 1/8$	5.60	$8 1/8$	7.43
$1/4$	0.23	$2 1/4$	2.06	$4 1/4$	3.89	$6 1/4$	5.72	$8 1/4$	7.54
$3/8$	0.34	$2 3/8$	2.17	$4 3/8$	4.00	$6 3/8$	5.83	$8 3/8$	7.66
$1/2$	0.46	$2 1/2$	2.29	$4 1/2$	4.11	$6 1/2$	5.94	$8 1/2$	7.77
$5/8$	0.57	$2 5/8$	2.40	$4 5/8$	4.23	$6 5/8$	6.06	$8 5/8$	7.89
$3/4$	0.69	$2 3/4$	2.51	$4 3/4$	4.34	$6 3/4$	6.17	$8 3/4$	8.00
$7/8$	0.80	$2 7/8$	2.63	$4 7/8$	4.46	$6 7/8$	6.29	$8 7/8$	8.12
1	0.91	3	2.74	5	4.57	7	6.40	9	8.23
$1 1/8$	1.03	$3 1/8$	2.86	$5 1/8$	4.69	$7 1/8$	6.52	$9 1/8$	8.34
$1 1/4$	1.14	$3 1/4$	2.97	$5 1/4$	4.80	$7 1/4$	6.63	$9 1/4$	8.46
$1 3/8$	1.26	$3 3/8$	3.09	$5 3/8$	4.91	$7 3/8$	6.74	$9 3/8$	8.57
$1 1/2$	1.37	$3 1/2$	3.20	$5 1/2$	5.03	$7 1/2$	6.86	$9 1/2$	8.69
$1 5/8$	1.49	$3 5/8$	3.31	$5 5/8$	5.14	$7 5/8$	6.97	$9 5/8$	8.80
$1 3/4$	1.60	$3 3/4$	3.43	$5 3/4$	5.26	$7 3/4$	7.09	$9 3/4$	8.92
$1 7/8$	1.71	$3 7/8$	3.54	$5 7/8$	5.37	$7 7/8$	7.20	$9 7/8$	9.03
2	1.83	4	3.66	6	5.49	8	7.32	10	9.14

Index

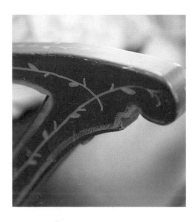